NOTES

ON THE

PARABLES OF OUR LORD

BY

RICHARD CHENEVIX TRENCH.

POPULAR EDITION

BAKER BOOK HOUSE

Grand Rapids, Michigan

ISBN: 0-8010-8774-0

First Printing, October 1948
Second Printing, August 1950
Third Printing, January 1953
Fourth Printing, January 1955
Fifth Printing, November 1958
Sixth Printing, March 1961
Seventh Printing, November 1963
Eighth Printing, November 1965
Ninth Printing, March 1967
Tenth Printing, October 1968
Eleventh Printing, October 1969
Twelfth Printing, September 1971
Thirteenth Printing, July 1973
Fourteenth Printing, July 1974
Fifteenth Printing, August 1975

PHOTOLITHOPRINTED BY CUSHING - MALLOY, INC.
ANN ARBOR, MICHIGAN, UNITED STATES OF AMERICA
1975

NOTES ON THE
PARABLES OF OUR LORD

PREFACE

Dean Trench's NOTES ON THE PARABLES retains first place among the works on the subject in the English language. It is unrivaled in its extensive and judicious use of the studies of others, ancient or contemporary. The author seems to have left little unexamined which might shed even a side-light on his theme. Trench's treatment of the parables is unsurpassed in depth of spiritual insight. It abounds in practical applications for lives of Christians and non-Christians, for the church and the world.

This *Popular Edition* has been prepared to remove the features which limited the usefulness of Trench's original work. Nearly one-third of the NOTES ON THE PARABLES, as it first made its appearance, consisted of notes in Greek, Latin, French, and German. These have been carefully translated and evaluated. Those judged valuable have been interwoven with the text or retained as notes in the English language. The detailed accounts of erroneous views and their refutations have been largely omitted. While the body of the work is given in very nearly the author's own words, those responsible for the preparation of this issue have not hesitated to make alterations in the interest of simplicity and lucidity. The result of this extensive study and revision is a volume which is more readily usable than the original, while it retains all the scholarliness of the larger edition.

Students of the Bible will be pleased that this well-known work is again available, this time in a more usable form. This issue, which is a reprint of the 1861 edition in a slightly altered form, likewise makes these studies available for members of Bible Classes and study groups. It is equally suited for the study and devotional reading of the individual Christian. In short, this widely-recognized exposition of the parables has now been made available to the general Christian public.

CONTENTS

Introductory Remarks:

Parables:

INTRODUCTORY REMARKS

CHAPTER I.

On the Definition of the Parable

THOSE who have had occasion to define a parable,[1] do not appear to have found it an easy task. Rather than attempt to add another definition to those already given, I will seek to note briefly what seems to me to distinguish it from the fable, the allegory, and such other forms of composition as most closely border on it.

1. Some have confounded the parable with the Æsopic fable, or drawn between them only a slight and hardly perceptible line of distinction. But the parable is constructed to set forth a spiritual truth; while the fable is essentially of the earth, and never lifts itself above the earth. The fable just reaches that pitch of morality which the world will understand and approve. But it has no place in Scripture, for the purpose of Scripture — namely, the awakening of man to a consciousness of a Divine original, and the education of the spiritual in him — excludes it. The two fables in the Old Testament (Judges ix. 8-15, and 2 Kings xiv. 9) do no impeach the universality of this rule, for in neither case is it God that is speaking. For the purposes of the fable, which are the recommendation and enforcement of the prudential virtues, examples taken from the world beneath us are admirably suited. The greatest of all fables, Reynard the Fox, affords ample illustration of this.

It belongs to the loftier standing point of the parable that it should be deeply earnest. Severe and indignant it may be, but it never jests with the calamities of men, however well deserved, and its indignation is that of holy love. In this raillery, the fabulist frequently indulges.[2] There is still another point of difference between the parable and the fable. Although it cannot be said that the fabulist intends to deceive, when he attributes reason and language to beasts and trees, yet the severer reverence for truth, belonging to the higher moral teacher, will not allow even of this sporting with the truth. The great Teacher in His parables allowed Himself in nothing marvellous or anomalous; He presents to us no speaking trees, or reasoning beasts.

2. The parable is also different from the myth. The mythic narrative presents itself not merely as the vehicle of the truth, but as being itself the truth; while in the parables we see the perfect distinctness between form and essence, shell and kernel. There is indeed a resemblance, when upon some old legend or myth there is thrust some spiritual significance, which is clearly an after-thought. For instance, Narcissus was to the later Platonists the symbol of man, casting himself forth into the world, expecting to find the good answering to his nature, but finding death instead. It was their aim hereby to put a moral life into mythology, so that it might maintain its ground against the new life of Christianity.

3. The parable is also clearly distinguishable from the proverb, though it is true that the words are sometimes used interchangeably in the New Testament. (Thus, Matt. xv. 14, 15.) This interchange has come to pass, partly because there is but one word in the Hebrew to signify both parable and proverb; and also, because the proverb, like the parable, very commonly rests upon some comparison, expressed or implied (2 Peter ii. 22). Or again, the proverb is often a concentrated parable; as for instance, "If the blind lead the blind, both shall fall into the ditch," might easily be extended into a parable.

4. The parable differs from the allegory, but it is more in form than in essence. In the allegory, there is a blending, an interpenetration of the thing signifying and the thing signified. It needs not, as the parable, an interpretation from without, for it contains its interpretation within itself, and as it proceeds,

that also proceeds, or at least is never far behind it. (The "Pilgrim's Progress" amply illustrates this.) Thus Isaiah v. 1-6, is a parble, the explanation being in ver. 7; while Psalm lxxx. 8-16, resting on the same image is an allegory. And as we have seen that many proverbs are concise parables, in like manner also, many are brief allegories. The eastern proverb, "The world is a carcass, and they who gather round it are dogs," interprets itself as it goes along; while the proverb spoken by our Lord, "Wheresoever the carcass is, there will the eagles be gathered together," gives no interpretation of itself.

To sum up all, the parable differs from the fable, by moving in a spiritual world, and never transgressing the actual order of natural things — from the myth, because in that there is an unconscious blending of the deeper meaning with the outward symbol, the two remaining separate in the parable — from the proverb, inasmuch as it is longer carried out, and not merely accidentally but necessarily figurative — from the allegory, by comparing one thing *with* another, and not transferring, as the allegory, the properties of one *to* the other.

CHAPTER II.

On Teaching by Parables

NO ONE can deny, without doing great violence to our Lord's words as recorded in Matt. iii. 10-15; Mark iv, 11, 12; Luke viii. 9, 10, that it was sometimes his purpose in teaching by parables, to withdraw from certain of his hearers the knowledge of truths which they were unworthy or unfit to receive. If not, where would be the fulfilment of the prophecy in Isaiah vi. 10? It is not that by the command, "Make the heart of this people fat," we need understand that any peculiar hardening passed upon them, but that the Lord having constituted as the righteous law of his moral government, that sin should produce moral insensibility, declared that he would allow the law in their case to take its course. The fearful curse of sin is, that it has ever the tendency to reproduce itself, that he who sows in sin reaps in spiritual darkness, which delivers him over again to worse sin.

But, notwithstanding this, we may assume as certain, that the general aim of our Lord in teaching by parables, was either to illustrate or to prove, and thus to make clearer, the truths which he had in hand. Or to *prove*, I say; the parable, or other analogy to spiritual truth appropriated from the world of nature or man, is not merely illustration, but, in the same sort, proof. For the power of such analogies lies in the harmony unconsciously felt by all, and by deeper minds plainly perceived, between the natural and spiritual worlds; the world of nature being throughout a witness for the world of spirit. To lovers of truth the things on earth are copies of the things in heaven. Rather, instead of being happily, but arbitrarily, chosen illustrations, do they belong to one another, the type and the thing typified, by an inward necessity. It is not a happy accident that the analogy of husband and wife sets forth the mystery of Christ's relation to His elect Church; but rather the earthly relation is only a lower form of the heavenly, on which it rests, and of which it is the utterance. The Lord is king, not borrowing this title from the kings of the earth, but having lent His own title to them; and the "kingdom of God" is, in fact, a most literal expression; it Is rather the earthly kingdoms that are figures and shadows of the truth. The untended soil yielding thorns and briers, is ever a type of man's heart, which, if neglected, will bring forth *its* thorns and *its* briers; and the weeds that *will* mingle during the time of growth with the corn, and yet are separated from it at last, tell always the same tale of the present mingling and future sundering of righteous and the wicked. And so, also, in the decaying of the seed, and from that the rising of the fruitful ear, we see evermore the prophecy of the final resurrection — it is the same power putting itself forth upon meaner things. And thus, besides his written revelation, God has an elder, and one without which we cannot conceive how that other could be made, for from this it appropriates all its signs of communication. The entire moral and visible world, with its kings and its subjects, its sun and its moon, its sleeping and its waking, and all its variety of operations, is one mighty parable.

It is true that men are ever in danger of losing "the key of knowledge" which opens the portals of this palace; and indeed in all, save in the one Man, there is more or less of the dulled ear, and the filmed eye. There is none to whom nature tells all that she has to tell. Now, the whole of Scripture, with its constant use of figurative language, is a re-awakening of man to the mystery of nature, and giving back to him the key of knowledge; and this comes out in its highest form, but by no means exclusively, in the parables. These were a calling of attention to the spiritual facts which underlie all processes of nature, all human institutions. Christ moved in the midst of what seemed to the eye of sense an old and worn-out world, and it became new at his touch; for it told to man the inmost secrets of his being, and he found that of these two worlds, without him, and within, each threw a light and glory on the other.

For the possibility of a real teaching by parables, rests on this — that this is God's world, the same God who is leading us into spiritual truth, and that being God's it is a sharer in his great redemption. We must not forget, indeed, that nature in its present state contains but a prophecy of its coming glory; it "groaneth and travaileth"; it is suffering under our curse. Yet suffering thus, it has more fitting symbols to declare to us our disease and misery, and the processes of their healing. It has its storms, and wildernesses, its lions and adders, by these interpreting to us death and all that leads to death, no less than by its more beneficent workings life and all that tends to the restoring and maintaining of life.

Still, not the less does it come short of its full purpose and meaning. It does not always speak out, in distinct accents, of God's truth and love. One day it will be translucent with the divine idea which it embodies, and which even now shines through it so wondrously. For no doubt the end will be, not the abolition of this nature, but the glorifying of it, — that which is now nature (*natura*), always, as the word expresses it, struggling to the birth, will then be born; and the new creation will be as the glorious child born out of the world-long throes of the old. But at present, the natural world, through its share in man's fall, has lost in some measure its fitness for the expressing of his higher condition. Obnoxious to change, tainted with decay, all earthly things are weak and temporary, when they undertake to set forth things strong and eternal. They break down under the weight that is laid upon them. The father, unlike that heavenly Father, chastens after his own pleasure. The word of God, which liveth and abideth forever, is set forth by the seed which itself perishes at last. There is something exactly analogous to all this, in the personages mentioned in

Scripture, as typical of the Divine Man. Through their sins and imperfections they all break down, sooner or later. For instance, few would deny the typical character of Solomon. Yet all that gorgeous forecasting of the coming glory is vouchsafed to us only for an instant. Even before his reign is done, we lose the brightness of the coloring, the distinctness of the outline.

Again, we see some men, in whom there is but a single point in their history which brings them into typical relation to Christ; such was Jonah, the type of the Resurrection: or persons whose lives at one moment and another seem to stand out as symbolic; Samson will suggest himself as one of these. It is scarcely possible to believe that Judges xiv. 14 and xvi. 30 mean nothing more than is contained in the letter. And so it is in every case, for somewhere or other every man is a liar; he is false, that is, to the Divine idea, which he was meant to embody. So that of the truths of God in the language of men, which language, of course, includes man's acts as well as his words, it may truly be said, "We have this treasure in earthen vessels." No doubt it was this consciousness of the drawbacks that attend all our means of communication, that caused the mystics to press the idea that we should seek to abstract ourselves from all images of things, and that to raise ourselves to the contemplation of pure and naked truth is the height of spiritual attainment. It has been said that as the kernel of the seed while in the earth disengages itself from the outer coating, and alone fructifies while the husk perishes, so in the seed of God's word, deposited in man's heart, the sensible form must fall off, that the inner germ may germinate. But, we must observe, the outer covering is not to fall off and perish, but to become glorified. Man is body and soul, and the truth has, for him, need of a body and soul likewise; it is well that he should be able to distinguish between the two, but not that he should seek to kill the body, that he may get at the soul.

The teacher, who would find his way to the hearts and understandings of his hearers, will never keep down the parabolical element of his teaching,[1] but will make as frequent use of it as he can. To do this effectually, will need a fresh effort of his own; for while all language is more or less figurative, yet long use has worn out the freshness of the stamp, so that, to create a powerful impression, language must be cast into novel forms, as was done by our Saviour. He gave no doctrine in an abstract form, no skeleton of truth, but clothed them all, as it were, with flesh and blood. He acted Himself as He declared to His apostles they must act (Matt. xiii. 52) ; He brought forth out of His treasure things new and old; by the help of the old, making intelligible the new. And thus in His own example He has given us the secret of all effectual teaching.

Had our Lord spoken naked spiritual truth, how many of His words would have entirely passed away from the hearts and memories of His hearers. But being imparted to them in this form, under some lively image, or in some brief but interesting narrative, they awakened attention, and excited inquiry; or even if, at the time, the truth did not find an entrance into the mind, His words laid up in the memory, were, to many that heard Him, like the money of another country, of which they knew not the value, but which yet was ready for use when they reached that land. When the Spirit brought all things to their remembrance, He quickened the forms of truth, which they already possessed, with the power and spirit of life. Gradually, the meanings of what they had heard, unfolded themselves. And thus must it ever be with all true knowledge, which is not the communication of information, but the planting seeds of truth, which shall take root in the new soil, and striking their roots downward, and sending their branches upward, shall grow into goodly trees.

We may also notice, that besides the spoken, there is much of acted, parable in Scripture. Every type is a *real* parable. The whole Levitical constitution, with its outer court, its holiest of all, its sacrifices, and all its ordinances, is declared to be such in the Epistle to the Hebrews (ix. 9). The wanderings of the children of Israel have ever been regarded as a parable of the spiritual life. We have, also, parabolic persons, who represented One higher and greater than themselves; men, who by their actions and sufferings were unconsciously drawing lines which another should hereafter fill up, as Abraham casting out Hagar (Gal. iv. 30), Jonah in the whale's belly, David in his hour of agony (Ps. 22). And, in a narrower circle, how often has God chosen that His servants should teach by an acted parable in order to make a more lasting impression. This will be seen in the conduct of Jeremiah; he breaks a potter's vessel (xix. 1-11); he wears a yoke (xxvii. 2, xxviii. 10); he redeems a field in pledge (xxxii. 6-15). All these acts were symbolical. And as God chooses that His servants shall teach by these means, so does He teach *them* by the same. Not by His word alone, does He teach His prophets, but the great truths of His kingdom pass before their eyes incorporated in symbols. They are indeed, and eminently, *seers.* This was perhaps more true of Ezekiel and Zechariah than of any others. We have an example of the same teaching in St. Peter's vision (Acts x. 9-16), and throughout all the visions of the Apocalypse. Nay, we might venture to affirm that so it was with the greatest truth, that which includes all others — the manifestation of God in the flesh. This, inasmuch as it was a making visible the invisible, a teaching not by doctrine, but by the embodied doctrine of a divine life, was the most glorious of all parables.

Our Lord's parables are found only in the three first Gospels; that of St. John containing allegories (x. 1; xv. 1). The gospel of St. Matthew was written originally for Jewish readers, and mainly for those of Palestine; and its leading purpose was to show that Jesus was the promised Messiah — the expected king of the Jews — the son of David; the parables recorded by him are concerning the kingdom, in harmony with the theocratic spirit of his Gospel. The main purpose of Luke was to show, not that Jesus was the king of the Jews, but the Saviour of the world; and therefore he traces our Lord's descent not merely from David, but from Adam. He, the chosen companion of the Apostle of the Gentiles, wrote his Gospel originally for Gentile readers; and, therefore, has been most careful to record the Lord's declarations concerning God's free mercy — that there is no departure from God so wide as to preclude a return. In this view, the three parables in chap. xv. are especially characteristic. St. Mark has but one parable peculiar to himself, namely, that of the seed growing by itself (iv. 26), and there is nothing in his record, I believe, to demand special notice.

CHAPTER III.

On the Interpretation of Parables

EACH one of the parables is like a casket, itself of exquisite workmanship, but in which jewels richer than itself are laid up; or like fruit, which, however lovely to look upon, is yet more delectable in its inner sweetness. To find, then, the golden key at the touch of which the casket shall reveal its treasures, to open this fruit so that nothing of its hidden kernel shall be lost, has ever been regarded as a matter of high concern. In the interpretation of the parable, the question, how much is significant? is one which has given rise to the most opposite theories. Some have gone a great way in saying, This is merely drapery, and not the vehicle of essential truth. Chrysostom continually warns against pressing too anxiously all the circumstances of a parable, and so also is it with Theophylact and Origen. It has been said that the parable and its interpretation are as a plane and a globe, which, though brought into contact, yet touch each other but in one point. On the other hand, Augustine, though sometimes laying down the same principle, frequently extends the interpretation through all the minutest fibres of the narrative. And in modern times, the followers of Cocceius have been particularly earnest in affirming all parts of a parable to be significant. It may well be considered whether those interpreters who claim that much of a parable is simply ornament, have not run into an extreme. It is quite true, as they say, that a knife is not all edge, nor a harp all strings. It is true, also, that in the other scheme of interpretation, there is danger lest a love for the exercise of ingenuity on the part of the interpreter, and admiration of the ingenuity so exercised on the part of the readers and hearers, may cause it to be forgotten that sanctification of the heart through the truth is the main purpose of all Scripture.

Yet, on the other hand, there is a shallow spirit ever ready to empty Scripture of the depth of its meaning, to exclaim, "This means nothing, this circumstance is not to be pressed;" and thus saying, we may fail to draw out from the Word of God all the riches therein contained; we may fail to admire the wisdom with which the type was constructed to correspond with its antitype. And still further, of those who start with the principle that much is to be set aside as nonessential, scarcely any two are agreed as to what actually is to be set aside; what one rejects, another retains, and the contrary. Besides, it is always observable that the more this system is carried out, the more the peculiar beauty of the parable disappears. When Storr, for instance, denies that the Prodigal leaving his father's house has any direct reference to man's departure from his heavenly Father, it is at once evident how much, both of pleasure and of instruction, is taken from us. It may also be remarked, in opposition to the interpretation of the parables in the gross, that when our Lord himself interpreted the two first which he delivered, those of the Sower and of the Tares, it is more than probable that he intended to furnish us with a key to the interpretation of them all. Now, in these, the moral application descends to some of the minutest details of the narrative.

It will help us much in this matter of determining what is essential and what not, if we first obtain fast hold of the central truth which the parable would set forth, and distinguish it in the mind as accurately as we can from all truths which border upon it; for only as seen from that middle point will the different parts appear in their true light. There is also this rule, that the introduction and application must be most carefully attended to These helps to interpretation are rarely or never lacking, though given in no fixed or formal manner; sometimes they are supplied by our Lord himself (Matt. xxii. 14; xxv. 13) ; sometimes by

the inspired narrators of His words (Luke xv. 1, 2; xviii. 1);
sometimes they precede the parable (Luke xviii. 9; xix. 11);
sometimes they follow (Matt. xxv. 13; Luke xvi. 9). The
parable of the Unmerciful Servant (Matt. xviii. 23) is furnished
with these helps to its right understanding, both at its opening
and at its close. So also are Matt. xx. 1-15, and Luke xii. 16-20.

Again we may observe that an interpretation, besides being
thus in accordance with its context, must be so without the use
of any very violent means; even, as generally, the interpretation
must be easy — if not always easy to be discovered, yet being
discovered, easy. For it is here as with the laws of Nature:
genius may be needful to discover the law, but being discovered
it throws back light upon itself, and commends itself unto all.
Again, as it is the proof of the law that it explains *all* the
phenomena, so it is tolerable evidence that we have found the
right interpretation of a parable, if it leave none of the main
circumstances unexplained.

Once more — the parables are not to be made first sources of
doctrine. Doctrines otherwise grounded may be illustrated, or
even further confirmed by them; but it is not allowable to constitute doctrines first by their aid. For from the literal to the
figurative, from the clearer to the more obscure, has ever been
recognized as the law of Scripture interpretation. This rule,
however, has been often forgotten, and controversialists, looking
around for arguments with which to sustain some weak position,
often invent for themselves supports in these. Thus Faustus
Socinus argues from the parable of the Unmerciful Servant, that
as the king pardoned his servant merely on his petition, so in the
same way God, without requiring sacrifice or intercessor, pardons
His debtors simply on the ground of their prayers. Socinus
here sins against another rule of Scripture interpretation, as of
common sense, which is, that we are not to expect, *in every
place,* the whole circle of Christian truth to be fully stated, and

that no conclusion may be drawn from the absence of a doctrine from one passage which is clearly stated in others.

But the greatest sinners against this rule, namely, that the parables are not to be made first sources of doctrine, were the Gnostics[1] and Manicheans, but especially the former. They only came to the Scripture to find an outer Christian coloring for a system essentially anti-Christian. They came, not to draw *out* of Scripture its meaning, but to thrust *into* Scripture their own (all of which very nearly repeats itself in Swedenborg). To sustain their doctrine, they were obliged to abandon the literal portions of Scripture; their only refuge was in the figurative, in those which might receive more interpretations than one; such perhaps they migh bend to their purposes. And as it was with the Gnostics, so was it with those sects of a later day, the Cathari and Bogomili.[2] They too found in the parables no teaching of sin and grace, no truths of the kingdom of God, but fitted to them the speculations about the creation, the origin of evil, the fall of angels, which they had themselves framed. Thus, in the parable of the Unjust Steward, they made Satan the chief steward over God's house, deposed from his high position, and drawing after him other angels with the suggestion of lighter tasks, and relief from the burden of their imposed duties.

There is another theory concerning the interpretation of the parables, held by Cocceius and his followers of what we may call the historico-prophetical school. By the parables, they say, and so far they are right, are declared the mysteries of the kingdom of God. Understanding these words — the kingdom of God — in far too exclusive a sense, they find in every one of the parables a part of the history of that kingdom's progressive development in the world, to the remotest times. They will not allow that any are merely for exhortation, for reproof, for instruction in righteousness. In the words of one of their number: —"The parables connect themselves with certain fixed periods of the progressive development of the Gospel of the kingdom, and as soon as these periods are completed, lose themselves in the very completion," that is, like all other fullfilled prophecy. Prophetical, no doubt, many of the parables are, for they declare how the new element of life, which the Lord was bringing into men's hearts and into the world, would work — the little mustard seed should grow to a great tree. But they do not declare so much the *facts* as the *laws* of the kingdom. Only a few are historico-prophetical. In the Wicked Husbandmen, for example, there is a clear prophecy of the death of Christ; and in the Marriage of the King's Son, there is also a clear announcement of the destruction of Jerusalem, and the transfer of the privileges of the kingdom of God from the Jews to the Gentiles.

CHAPTER IV.

On Other Parables Besides Those in the Scriptures

IT HAS been denied by some, but against all testimony, that the method of teaching by parables was current among the Jews before our Saviour's time. To this they had been mainly led by the fear lest it should detract from His glory, to suppose that He had availed Himself of a manner of teaching already in use. But if Christianity is indeed the world-religion, it must gather into one all dispersed rays of light; it must appropriate to itself all elements of truth which are anywhere scattered abroad, claiming thus its own. Our blessed Lord so spake, as that His doctrine, according to its outward form, should commend itself to His countrymen. Thus He appealed to proverbs in common use among them. He used the terms which they had employed, but all His words being creative, He breathed into them also a new spirit of life. The prayer, "Thy kingdom come," formed already a part of the Jewish liturgy, yet not the less was it a new prayer on the lips of all who had realized in any measure the idea of the kingdom, and what was signified by the coming of that kingdom, as He first had enabled them to realize it. In like manner it is not to be doubted that a proselyte was in the Jewish schools entitled "a new creature," and his passing over to Judaism was called "a new birth;" yet these terms were probably used to express a change only in his outward relations — that his kinsmen were his no more; it remained for Christ and His apostles to appropriate them to the higher mysteries of the kingdom of heaven.

It is also certain that the use of parables or briefer comparisons to illustrate doctrines, was eminently in use among the Jewish teachers. Hillel and Schammai were the most illustrious

21

teachers by parables before the time of our Saviour; R. Meir immediately after. With this last, as tradition goes, the power of inventing parables notably declined. I will quote some of the best Jewish parables which I have met with. The following is occasioned by a question which has arisen, namely, Why the good so often die young? It is answered, that God foresees that if they lived they would fall into sin. "To what is this like? It is like a king who, walking in his garden, saw some roses which were yet buds, breathing an ineffable sweetness. He thought, If these shed such sweetness while yet they are buds, what will they do when they are fully blown? After a while, the king entered the garden anew, thinking to find the roses now blown, and to delight himself with their fragrance; but arriving at the place, he found them pale and withered, and yielding no smell. He exclaimed with regret, Had I gathered them while yet tender and young, and while they gave forth their sweetness, I might have delighted myself with them, but now I have no pleasure in them. The next year the king walked in his garden, and finding rosebuds scattering fragrance, he commanded his servants, Gather them, that I may enjoy them before they wither, as last year they did." The next is ingenious enough, though a notable specimen of Jewish self-righteousness: — "A man had three friends: being summoned to appear before the king, he was terrified, and looked for an advocate; the first, whom he had accounted the best, altogether refused to go with him; another replied that he would accompany him to the door of the palace, but could not speak for him; the third, whom he had held in least esteem, appeared with him before the king, and pleaded for him so well as to procure his deliverance. So every man has three friends, when summoned by death before God, his Judge: the first, whom he most prized, his money, will not go with him a step; the second, his friends and kinsmen, accompany him to the tomb, but no further, nor can they deliver him in the judgment; while the third, whom he held in least esteem, the Law and good works, appear with him before the King, and deliver him from condemnation." How different is this view of the Law as an advocate with the Judge, from that given by our Lord (Matt. v. 25, 26), who compares it to an adversary dragging us before a tribunal where we are certain to be worsted!

There is a fine one of the fox, who seeing the fish in great trouble, darting hither and thither, while the stream was being drawn with nets, proposed to them to leap on dry land. This is put in a Rabbi's mouth, who, when the Græco-Syrian kings were threatening with death all who observed the law, was counselled by his friends to abandon it. There are besides these, a multitude of briefer ones, deserving the title of similitudes rather than of parables. Thus, the death common to all, and the doom after death so different to each, is likened to a king's retinue entering a city at a single gate, but afterward lodged within it very differently, according to their several dignity. In another it is shown how body and soul are partners in sin, and so will justly be partners in punishment. Thus: A mortal king assigned to an excellent garden in which were ripe fruits, two keepers, a lame man, and a blind man. The lame man seeing the fruit, persuaded the bind man to take him on his shoulders, so that he might pluck, and they both might eat, etc.

The resemblance which is seen between some of the Jewish parables and those related by our Lord, is merely such as must needs have found place, when the same external life, and the same outward nature, were used as the common storehouse from whence images and examples were drawn alike by all. The following is one of the best of those which pretend to any similarity with His, and has been sometimes likened to that part of the Marriage of the King's Son which relates to the wedding garment. "The Rabbis have delivered what follows, on Eccl. xii. 7, where it is written, 'The spirit shall return unto God who gave it.' He gave it to thee unspotted, see that thou restore it unspotted to Him again. It is like a mortal king, who distributed royal vestments to his servants. Then those that were wise, folded them carefully up, and hid them by in the wardrobe; but those that were foolish went their way, and, clothed in these garments, engaged in their ordinary work. After a while the king required his garments again; the wise returned them white as they had received them; but the foolish, soiled and stained. Then the king was well pleased with the wise, and said, Let the vestments be laid up in the wardrobe, and let these depart in peace; but he was angry with the foolish, and said, Let the vestments be given to be washed, and those servants be cast into prison: — so will the Lord do with the bodies of the righteous, as it is written, Isa. lvii. 2; with their souls, 1 Sam. xxv. 29; but with the bodies of the wicked, Isa. xlviii. 22, lvii. 21; and with their souls, 1 Sam. xxv. 29." But how slight the resemblance!

Thus much in regard of the Jewish parables. Among the Fathers of the Christian Church, there are not many, as far as I am aware, who have professly constructed parables for the setting forth of spiritual mysteries. Eadmer, a diciple of Anselm, has preserved a sort of basket of fragments from his sermons and his table-talk. Far better are those interspersed through the Greek religious romance of the seventh or eight century, *Barlaam and Josaphat,* ascribed, though I believe without sufficient grounds, to St. John of Damascus, and often printed with his works. Those which are entitled parables in the writings of St. Bernard, although containing much of beauty and instruction, are rather allegories than parables. But if parables, professedly such, are not of frequent occurrence in the early Church writers, the parabolical element is, notwithstanding, very prominent in their teaching. For instance, in the writings of St. Augustine, one is only perplexed amid the endless variety what instances to select: but we may take this one as an example. He is speaking of the Son of God and the sinner in the same world, and appearing under the same conditions of humanity. "But," he proceeds, "how great a difference there is between the prisoner in his dungeon and the visitor that has come to see him. They are both within the walls of the dungeon: one who did not know might suppose them under equal restraint, but one is the compassionate visitor who can use his freedom when he will, the other is fast bound there for his offences. So great is the difference between Christ, the compassionate visitor of man, and man himself, the criminal in bondage for his offences." Chrysostom, too, is very rich in such similitudes; as for instance, when speaking of the exaltation of outward nature, the redemption of the creature which shall accompany the manifestation of the sons of God, he says, "To what is the creation like? It is like a nurse that has brought up a royal child, and when he ascends his paternal throne, she too rejoices with him, and is partaker of the benefit." But the field here opening before us, is too wide to enter on. I will not deny myself the pleasure, however, of transcribing the following parable from H. de Sto. Victore. "A certain father drove out his rebellious son with much seeming rage, that he might thus learn humility. But persisting in his obstinacy, his mother, according to a secret plan, is sent by the father, that, not as if sent thus, but as if led by her own affection, she may soothe him by her gentleness, incline him to humility, declare that his father is greatly angered, yet promise to intercede, say that his father cannot be appeased except by great entreaties, but engage to undertake his cause herself, and to bring the affair to a happy termination." The mother, here, he presently explains as divine Grace.

One Persian parable, too, I will quote for its deep significance. "Mankind cannot be better compared than to a man who, fleeing from an enraged elephant, goes down into a well; he is caught on two boughs which cover its mouth, and his feet are placed upon something which projects from the interior of the well — it is four serpents, who put their heads out of their dens; he perceives at the bottom of the well a dragon, which, with open maw, awaits only the moment of his fall to devour him. His attention is turned to the two boughs, from which he is suspended, and he sees at their starting-point two rats, the one black, the other white, which cease not to gnaw them. Another object, however, presents itself to his notice; it is a beehive filled with bees: he applies himself to eating of their honey, and the pleasure he finds in it causes him to forget the serpents on which rest his feet, the rats which gnaw the branches, and the danger which every moment threatens him of becoming the prey of the dragon. His folly and delusion cease only with his life. This well — 'tis the world filled with perils and miseries; the four serpents are the four humors whose mixture forms our body, but which, when their equilibrium is destroyed, become so many fatal poisons; the two rats, black and white, are day and night, whose succession consumes our life; the dragon is the inevitable limit which awaits us all; the honey, finally, is those pleasures whose false sweetness allures and misleads us."

PARABLES

CHAPTER I.

THE SOWER

Matt. xiii. 3-8, and 18-23; Mark iv. 3-8, and 14-20; Luke viii. 5-8, and 11-15.

IT IS evidently the purpose of St. Matthew to present to his readers the parables recorded in the thirteenth chapter of his Gospel, as the first which the Lord spoke; with this of the Sower he commenced a manner of teaching which he had not hitherto used. We have not anywhere else in the Gospels so rich a group of parables assembled together. The only passage that will bear comparison is chapters xv. and xvi. of St. Luke, where there are recorded five parables that were all apparently spoken on the same occasion.

St. Matthew tells us, that "Jesus went out from the house," probably at Capernaum, which was the city where he commonly dwelt after his open ministry began — "his own city" (Matt. ix. 1), and which was close by the sea-shore; and going out, he "sat down by the sea-side," that is, by the lake of Genesareth. This lake (now Bahr Tabaria) goes by many names in the Gospels. It is often called simply "the sea," or, "the Sea of Galilee,"[1] or, "the Sea of Tiberias," though indeed it was an inland lake of no very great extent, being but about sixteen miles in length, and no more than six in breadth.

The Lord lifted, it may be, his eyes, and saw at no great distance an husbandman scattering his seed in the furrows.[2] We find this comparison of the teacher and the taught to the sower and the soil, of very frequent recurrence, not merely in Scripture (1 Pet. i. 23; 1 John iii. 9), but in the works of all the wiser heathen, such as Aristotle, Cicero, Plutarch, and others. While all teaching that is worthy the name, is as seed, with a power to take root in the hearts of those that hear it, in a much

29

higher sense must this be true of the words which *He* spake
who was himself the Seminal Word which he communicated.
I cannot doubt that the Lord intended to set himself forth as
the chief sower of the seed. His entrance into the world was
a going forth to sow; the word of the kingdom was his seed; the
hearts of men his soil.

*And when he sowed, some seeds fell by the wayside [and it
was trodden down], and the fowls came and devoured them up.*
Some, that is, fell on the hard road, where it could not sink
down in the earth, but lay exposed to the feet of passers by, till
at length it became an easy prey to the birds, which in the
East follow in large flocks the husbandman, to gather up, if
possible, the scattered seed-corn. Christ thus explains this:
*When any one heareth the word of the kingdom, and under-
standeth it not, then cometh the wicked one, and catcheth away
that which was sown in his heart.* The words which St. Matthew
alone records, *and understandeth it not,* are very important for
the comprehending of what this first state of mind and heart is,
in which the Word of God is unproductive of any effect. The
man understands it not; he does not recognize himself as standing in any relation to the word, or to the kingdom of grace
which that word proclaims. All that speaks of man's connection
with an invisible world, all that speaks of sin, of redemption,
of holiness, is unintelligible, and wholly without significance. He
has exposed his heart as a common road to every evil influence
of the world, till it has become hard as a pavement.[3] Besides
all this, there is one always watching to take advantage of this
evil condition of the soil, and he sends his ministers in the
shape of evil thoughts, worldly lusts, etc., and by their help
immediately taketh away the word that was sown in their hearts.
And the Lord concludes, *This is he that receiveth seed by the
way-side.*

*Some fell upon stony places, where they had not much earth,
and forthwith they sprung up, because they had no deepness of*

earth; *and when the sun was up, they were scorched, and be-cause they had no root they withered away.*[4] A soil mingled with stones is not meant by the expression, "stony places," for this would not hinder the roots from striking downward. But what is meant is a ground where a thin coating of mould covered the surface of a rock. Christ then says, *They on the rock are they which, when they hear, receive the word with joy; and these have no root, which for a while believe, and in time of temptation fall away.* We have here a state of mind not stubbornly repelling the truth, but lacking in earnestness; the same spirit which was in the minds of the great multitudes who followed Jesus, to whom he turned and told in the strongest language what discipleship to him involved (Luke xiv. 25-33). *So hath he not root in himself,*[5] *but dureth for a while, for when tribulation*[6] *or persecution ariseth because of the word, by and by he is offended.* The troubles and afflictions which would have strengthened a true faith, cause a merely temporary faith to fail. The having the inward root answers to having a foundation on a rock (Matt. vii. 25), and the image itself is not an unfrequent one in Scripture (Eph. iii. 17; Col. ii. 7). Illustrations may be taken of this enduring faith from Heb. x. 34, and 2 Cor. iv. 17, 18. Demas on the other hand lacked that root.

Thirdly — *Some fell among thorns, and the thorns sprung up and choked it,*[7] so that *it yielded no fruit.* Here there was no lack of soil, perhaps good soil; but what was deficient was a careful husbandry, the extermination of thorns and weeds. Christ says — *He also that received seed among the thorns, is he that heareth the word, and the cares of this world and the deceitfulness of riches choke the word, and he becometh unfruitful.* In this case, the profession of a spiritual life is retained, but the power of religion is by degrees eaten out. This is to be attributed to two things: the cares of this world, and its pleasures;[8] these are the thorns and briers that strangle the life of the soul. While that which God promises is felt to be good, but also what the

world promises is felt to be equally good, there will be an
attempt made to serve God and Mammon (Luke xxi. 34;
1 Tim. vi. 9).

But *Other fell into good ground, and brought forth fruit,
some an hundred fold, some sixty fold, some thirty fold.* The
return of a hundred for one is not unheard of in the East
(Gen. xxvi. 12). Herodotus says that two hundred fold was a
common return in the plain of Babylon, and sometimes three.
We learn that *He that receiveth seed into the good ground, is
he that heareth the word, and understandeth it, which also bear-
eth fruit . . .* or with St. Luke, *That on the good ground are
they, who in an honest and good heart, having heard the word,
keep it, and bring forth fruit with patience.* How can any heart
be called *good,* before the Word and the Spirit have made it so?[9]
"Being of the truth," "doing truth," "having the soil of a good
and honest heart," all mean the same thing, viz., a receptivity
for the truth. The preaching of the Gospel may be likened to
the scattering of sparks; where they find tinder, they fasten and
kindle into a flame. So when Christ preached the word, there
were, as there still are, two divisions of men. One was of the
false-hearted, who called good evil, and evil good, self-excusers
and self-justifiers, such as were the Scribes and Pharisees for the
most part. The other class were sinners too, but yet acknowledg-
ing their sins, and having no wish to alter the everlasting relations between right and wrong. Such were the Matthews and the
Zaccheuses. Nathaniel would be yet a more perfect specimen
— a man of a simple, earnest, truthful nature, who had been
faithful to the light which he had — who had not resisted God's
preparation for imparting to him His best gift — for we must
keep in mind that the good soil comes as much from God as the
seed.

I suppose that the different measures of prosperity given in
the return, indicate different degrees of fidelity in those that
receive the word. The words, *Take heed, therefore, how ye*

hear; for whosoever hath, to him shall be given, and whosoever hath not, from him shall be taken even that which he seemeth to have, are very important. The disciples might have been in danger of supposing that these four conditions of heart were permanently fixed. The warning, *Take heed how ye hear,* obviates the possibility of such a mistake, for it tells us that according as we hear and receive the word, so will its success be — that even for those who have brought themselves into an evil condition, recovery is still, through the grace of God, possible. For, whilst it is true that there is such a thing as laying waste the very soil, yet, on the other hand, the hard soil may again become soft — the shallow soil deep — the soil beset with thorns clear. For the heavenly seed, if acted on by the soil, also reacts more mightily upon it (Jer. xxiii. 29).

CHAPTER II.

THE TARES

Matt. xiii. 24-30, and 36-43.

T HE KINGDOM of heaven is likened unto a man that sowed good seed in his field. He that sowed good seed, is the Son of man.[1] This is the most frequent title by which our Lord designates Himself, though it is never given Him by any other, except by Stephen (Acts vii. 56), to whom it would seem probable the glorified Saviour appeared bodily. *The field is the world.*[2] This parable relates, as our Lord tells us at the beginning, to the kingdom of heaven, or the church. The word *world* need not perplex us; it *was* the world, and therefore was rightly called so, till this seed was sown in it, but thenceforth was the world no longer. No narrower word would have sufficed for Him, in whose prophetic eye the word of the Gospel was contemplated as going forth, to be sown in every part of the great field of the nations.

But while man slept, his enemy came and sowed tares among the wheat, and went his way. Our Lord here alluded to a form of malice which was familiar to his hearers. It involved little risk, and yet accomplished great mischief. A modern writer affirms the same to be now practised in India. In Ireland, an outgoing tenant, in spite, sowed wild oats in the fields which he was leaving, and it was next to impossible to exterminate them. The phrase *while men slept* is equivalent to "at night," and means nothing more.

The enemy that sowed (the tares) *is the devil,* so that we see Satan here, not as he works beyond the limits of the church, but in his malignity, mimicking and counterworking the work of Christ. We may here also notice the increasing distinctness

35

(in comparison with the Old Testament) with which the doctrine of Satan's agency and of his active hostility to the blessedness of man is brought out; as the lights become brighter, the shadows become deeper. It was not until the Son of man actually appeared on the stage of the world, that Satan came distinctly forward upon it also. And instead of hearing less of Satan, as the mystery of the kingdom of God unfolds itself, in the last book of Scripture, which details the fortune of the church till the end of time, he is brought in as more openly working than in any other.

It is observable, too, that Satan is spoken of as *his* enemy; for here the great conflict is spoken of as rather between Satan and the Son of man, than between Satan and God. (Compare Gen. iii. 15.) It was part of the plan of redemption that the victory over evil should be a moral, rather than a physical, triumph. It was important, then, that man, who lost the battle, should also win it (1 Cor. xv. 21). Satan is all darkness; in him is no light. God is all light, and in Him is no darkness at all. Man holds a middle ground. In him, light and darkness are struggling. Herein lies the possibility of redemption, because his will is only perverted; Satan's will is inverted, for he has said, what it is never possible for a man *fully* to act upon, "Evil be thou my good;" and therefore, as far as we can see, restoration is impossible for him. This thought, also, is full of instruction, that wheat and tares are not seeds of different kinds, but that tares are a bastard wheat. This fact makes the image curiously adapted to the setting forth the origin of evil,[3] that it is not a generation, but a degeneration.—Having sown his tares, the enemy *went his way.* How often, in the church, the beginnings of evil have been scarcely discernible. The tares did not appear to be such till *the blade was sprung up, and brought forth fruit.* The difference between the wheat, and this lolium or tare, is only distinguishable when the ear is formed; thus fulfilling literally the Lord's words, "By their fruits ye shall know them." Augustine remarks that it is only the opposition of good which makes evil to appear. As there must be light, with which to contrast the darkness, height wherewith to measure depth, so there must be holiness to be grieved at unholiness. This is as true of each individual heart's experience as of the collective church.

So the servants of the householder came and said unto him, Sir, didst not thou sow good seed in thy field? from whence then hath it tares? These servants are not angels, but men who indeed had a righteous zeal for their master's honor; but it needed to be tempered and restrained (compare Luke ix. 54). The question, *Didst not thou sow good seed in thy field?* expresses well the surprise and perplexity which must have been felt by all, in the first ages especially, who were zealous for God, at the woeful appearance which the visible church presented. Where was the "glorious church, not having spot or wrinkle, or any such thing?" But the reply is, *An enemy hath done this.* It is attributed not to the imperfection which clings to every thing human, but to the distinct counterworking of the great spiritual enemy. In the question, *Wilt thou then that we go and gather them up?* the temptation to use outward power for the suppression of error finds utterance. Therefore he said, *Nay.* By this prohibition are doubtless forbidden all such measures for the excision of offenders as shall leave them no possibility for repentance.

Let both grow together until the harvest.[4] We learn from this, that evil is not to disappear before good, but to develop itself more fully, as on the other side good is to unfold itself more mightily also. Thus it will go on, until they stand face to face in the persons of Christ and Antichrist. It is clear that when Christ asserts that it is His purpose to make a complete separation at the end, He forbids, not the exercise of godly discipline, but any attempts to anticipate the final separation. At that time, He will give the command, not to these servants, but to the reapers —*his angels, and they shall gather out of his kingdom, all things that offend, and all which do iniquity.* The lot of the tares is to be gathered into bundles, and burned, or, as it here, the angels *shall cast them into the furnace of fire.* Augustine explains this gathering into bundles by the idea of "like to like;" "that is," "extortioners with extortioners, adulterers with adulterers, murderers with murderers, thieves with thieves, etc." The punishment by fire was one that was not in use among the Jews, but one with which they were not unacquainted. It was employed by the Chaldeans (Jer. xxix. 22, Dan. iii. 6). The wailing and gnashing of teeth are expressions of rage and impatience (Acts vii. 54).

Then shall the righteous shine forth[5] *as the sun in the kindom of their Father.* A glory shall be revealed *in* the saints; it shall not merely be brought to them. It shall be a glory which they before had, but which did not appear. That shall be the day of the manifestation of the sons of God; they shall be acknowledged as children of the Father of Lights (Jas. i. 17). Not till then shall be accomplished those glorious prophecies recorded in the Old Testament: "Henceforth there shall no more come into thee the uncircumcised and the unclean" (Isa. lii. 1) ; "Thy people also shall be all righteous" (Isa. lx. 21) ; compare Zech. xiv. 21; Isa. xxxv. 8; Joel iii. 17; Ezek. xxxvii. 21-27; Zeph. iii. 13.

CHAPTER III.

THE MUSTARD SEED

Matt. xiii. 31, 32; Mark iv. 30-32; Luke xiii. 18, 19.

THIS parable, and the one that follows, would seem, at first sight, merely repetition of the same truth; but upon inspection, essential differences appear. The other, of the leaven, is concerning the kingdom of God, which "cometh not with observation;" this is concerning the same kingdom, as it displays itself openly, and cannot be hid. That sets forth the power of the truth on the world brought in contact with it,—this the power of the truth to develop itself from within itself. The description of the small and slight beginnings and of the marvellous increase of the church is common to both.

The connection between this parable and all that has gone before, is thus traced by Chrysostom. In the parable of the Sower, the disciples had heard that only a fourth part of the seed sown had prospered; in the Tares, they had heard of the hindrances which beset even the part that remained. Lest they should be tempted to dispair, our Lord speaks these two parables for their encouragement.

The comparison of the growth of His kingdom to that of a tree, was one made familiar to His hearers from the Old Testament. The growth of a worldly kingdom had been set forth under this image (Dan. iv. 10-12; Ezek. xxxi. 3-9) ; as also that of the kingdom of God (Ps. lxxx. 8). We may also notice the reverence with which all antiquity was accustomed to look upon trees. The most accurate inquiries of naturalists seem to point out as the mustard tree of this parable, not that which goes by this name in Western Europe, but what is commonly called in Syria, Khardal. It is described as having a pleasant, though

39

strongly aromatic taste, like mustard. The mustard-seed is here chosen because of the proportion between the smallness of its seed and the greatness of the plant which unfolds from it. The Lord wishes to set before His disciples the fact, that His kingdom should be glorious in spite of its weak and despised beginning. Nor can I see anything so very ridiculous in the supposition that this seed was chosen on account of further qualities which it possessed; its fiery vigor, the fact that through being bruised, it gives out its best virtues, and all this in so small a compass, may have moved him to select this as an image of the doctrine of a crucified Redeemer, which, though a foolishness and a stumbling-block to some, should prove, to them that believed, "the power of God unto salvation." Nor is it his doctrine merely, but Christ himself that is the grain of mustard seed, for the kingdom of heaven, or the church, was originally enclosed in him, and from him unfolded itself.

This seed is, when cast into the ground, *the least of all seeds.* Although this is not literally true, yet the words "Small as a grain of mustard seed" were a proverbial expression among the Jews (Luke xvii. 6). The Koran reads—"Oh, my son, every matter, though it be of the weight of a grain of mustard seed," etc. The Son of man grew up in a despised province; he did not appear in public until his thirieth year; then taught for two or three years in neighboring villages, and occasionally at Jerusalem; made a few converts, chiefly among the poor and unlearned; and then falling into the hands of his enemies, died the shameful death of the cross; such, and so slight, was the commencement of the universal kingdom of God. The great schemes of this world have a proud beginning, a miserable end —like the towers of Babel; but the works of God, most of all His church, have a slight beginning, with gradual increase, and a glorious consummation. So it is with His kingdom also in every single heart.

The seed, *when it is grown, is the greatest among herbs, and becometh a tree, so that the birds of the air come and lodge in the branches thereof.* It is well known that in hot countries, as in Judea, the mustard tree attains a size never reached in colder latitudes. A traveller in Chili mentions the fact of riding on horseback under a tree of this kind. Maldonatus relates that in Spain the birds are exceedingly fond of the seed, so that at times he has seen them lighting in great numbers on the boughs. In the image of the birds flocking to the boughs of the tree, and there finding shelter and food (Ezek. xvii. 23), we are to recognize a prophecy of the refuge and defence there should be for all men in the church; how that multitudes should find here protection, as well as satisfaction for all the wants of their souls.

CHAPTER IV.

THE LEAVEN

Matt. xiii. 33; Luke xiii. 20, 21

THIS parable relates also to the marvellous increase of the
kingdom of God; and not merely its development from within itself, but its influence on the world which it touches on all
sides. The mustard-seed for a while does not attract observation,
but the active working of the leaven has been from the moment
that it was hidden in the lump. It is undoubtedly true, that
leaven is used most frequently in Scripture as the symbol of
something evil (1 Cor. v. 7; Luke xii. 1). Yet, because such
is its most frequent use, it is not necessary to interpret the
parable, as some do, as though it were a prophecy of the workings of the future mystery of inquity. In the present case, its
warmth, its penetrative energy, the power which a little of it has
to lend its savor and virtue to much with which it comes in
contact, are the chief points of comparison.

There is no need, then,[1] to take the parable in any other
than its obvious sense, namely, that it concerns the diffusion,
and not the corruptions, of the Gospel. By the leaven we are
to understand the word of the kingdom, which Word in its
highest sense Christ himself was. Of Him it was said, "He hath
no form nor comeliness, and when we shall see him, there is no
beauty that we should desire him;" but presently, "By his knowledge shall my righteous Servant justify many; he shall divide the
spoil with the strong" (Isa. liii. 2, 11, 12); and when He had
given of His life and spirit to the Apostles, they too, though poor
and unlearned, became the leaven of the world.

We see that the woman *took* the leaven from elsewhere to
mingle it with the lump; even such is the Gospel, a kingdom

43

not of this world (John xviii. 36). It was not the unfolding of any powers already existing in the world, but a new power brought from above;[2] not a philosophy, but a Revelation. This leaven is said to have been *hidden* in the mass. The renovation which God effects is ever thus, from the inward to the outward. In the early history of Christianity the leaven was effectually hidden. This is shown by the entire ignorance which heathen writers betray of all that was going forward a little below the surface of society, even up to the very moment (with slight exceptions) when the triumph of Christianity was at hand.

We cannot consider the words, *till the whole is leavened*, as less than a prophecy of final triumph of Christianity. We may also see in these words an assurance that the word of life, received into any single heart, shall not cease its working till it has brought the whole man into obedience to it, sanctifying him wholly, so that he shall be altogether a new creation in Christ Jesus. The parable sets forth the mystery of regeneration, both in its first act, which can be but once, as the leaven is but once hidden; and also in the consequent work of the Holy Ghost, which, as the working of the leaven, is continual and progressive.

CHAPTER V.

THE HID TREASURE

Matt. xiii. 44.

T HE KINGDOM of God is not merely a general, it is also an individual, thing. A man may dwell in a Christendom which has been leavened, and so in a manner share in the universal leavening; but more than this is needed, and more than this in every elect soul will find place. There will be a personal appropriation of the benefit, and we have the history of this in these two parables which follow. The two are each the complement of the other; so that as finders either of the pearl or the hid treasure, may be classed all who become partakers of the rich treasure, of the Gospel of Christ. One class is of those who feel that there must be some absolute good for man, and are, therefore, seeking everywhere for this good. Such are likened to the merchant who has the distinct purpose set before him of seeking goodly pearls. These are the fewest in number, but are, perhaps, the noblest converts to the truth. Again, there are others, who do not discover that there is an aim and a purpose for man's life, until the truth as it is in Jesus is revealed to them. Such are likened to the finder of the hid treasure, who stumbled upon it unawares. The joy of this last class—being the joy at the discovery of an unlooked-for treasure—is expressed.

The case of the Jews may illustrate the parable of the Pearl; though it cannot be fully carried out, for the most of them, although seeking the pearl, having a zeal for righteousness, yet when the pearl of great price was offered to them, were not willing to sell all—to renounce their self-righteousness, and all else that they held dear, that they might buy it. The Gentiles, on the contrary, at least most of them, came upon the treasure

45

unawares. Christ was found of them that sought him not. The case of Nathanael was of this kind. The Samaritan woman (John iv.) is a still more striking example. There must be in such characters a desire for the truth (though previously it may have slumbered in the soul), displaying itself in joyful acquiescence in it when revealed. On the other hand, we have a picture of a noble nature, seeking earnestly for the pearl of great price, in Augustine.

A writer on Oriental customs says, that in the East, on account of frequent changes in dynasties, and consequent revolutions, many rich men divide their goods into three parts: one they employ in commerce, or for their support; one they turn into jewels, which might be easily carried; and a third part they bury. The traveller in modern times often finds great difficulty in obtaining information about antiquities, owing to the jealousy of the neighboring inhabitants, who fear lest he is coming to carry away concealed hoards of wealth from among them. Often, too, a man abandoning his regular occupation, will devote himself to treaure-seeking, in the hope of growing suddenly rich (Job iii. 21; Prov. ii. 4).

Some draw a distinction between the field and the treasure, making the first to be the Scriptures, the second the knowledge of Christ.[1] To me the *field* rather represents the outer visible Church, as distinguished from the inward spiritual. He who recognizes the Church not as a human institute, but a divine, who has learned that God is in the midst of it, sees now that it is something beyond all earthly societies with which he has confounded it; and henceforth it is precious in his sight, even to its outermost skirts, for the sake of its inward glory, which is now revealed to his eyes. And as the man cannot have the treasure, and leave the field, so he cannot have Christ except in his Church; he cannot have Christ in his heart, and at the same time separate his fortunes from those of Christ's struggling, suffering Church. The treasure and the field go together.

But not to anticipate,—this treasure, *when a man hath found, he hideth*. If one hide the spiritual treasure, it will be not lest another should find it, but lest he himself should lose it. In the first moments that the truth is revealed to the soul, there may well be a fear lest the blessing should by some means escape from it; and this anxiety and the consequent precautions seem to be indicated here. Having thus secured it, the finder, *for joy thereof, goeth and selleth all that he hath, and buyeth that field.*2 It is in the strength of this joy that the finder of the spiritual treasure is enabled to go and sell all that he hath; all other things have no glory, "by reason of the glory which excelleth." Augustine says, in describing his conversion, "How sweet did it at once become to me, to want the sweetness of those toys! and what I feared to be parted from was now a joy to part with." Compare Phil. iii. 4-11. So, whenever any man renounces the thing that is closest to him—when the lover of money renounces his covetousness—and the lover of pleasure, his pleasure—then each is selling what he has that he may buy the field which contains the treasure. Compare Matt. xvi. 24; Mark ix. 43-48.

Some have found a difficulty in the circumstance that the finder of the treasure kept back from the owner of the field the knowledge of the fact. But to this objection, it seems a sufficient reply to say that not every part of his conduct who found the treasure is proposed for imitation, but only his earnestness in securing the treasure found, his fixed purpose to make it his own, and his prudence.

CHAPTER VI.

THE PEARL

Matt. xiii. 45, 46.

ALMOST all which would have been said on this parable, had it stood alone, has been anticipated in the previous one. *The kingdom of God is like unto a merchantman seeking goodly pearls.* To find them has been the object of his labors. He is one who has felt that man was not made in vain, that there must be a center of peace for him, who is determined not to rest until the good is found. Perhaps he does not yet know that it is but *one*, for at his starting he is seeking *many* goodly pearls.

We must keep in mind the great esteem in which the pearl was held in antiquity, so that there is record of almost incredible sums offered for single pearls, when perfect. A yellow or dusky tinge, or a want of entire smoothness or roundness, materially diminished their value. Origen observes that the fact of there being so many inferior pearls, adds an emphasis to the epithet here used. The theory of the formation of pearls, current in ancient times, is told by Origen. The fish conceived the pearl from the dew of heaven, and according to the quality of the dew, it was pure and round, or cloudy and deformed with specks. The merchant is seeking *goodly* pearls. Thus the one represented is not living for sensual objects. He has been, it may be, a seeker of wisdom, a philanthropist, a worshipper of the beautiful in nature or art—who has hoped to find his soul's satisfaction in these. But the pearl of price, which at length he finds— this pearl is the kingdom of God within a man—or the knowledge of Christ.

But when he had found it, he *went and sold all that he had, and bought it.* What this selling means, has been told in the

49

previous parable, and to understand what the buying means, we may compare Isa. lv. 1; Matt. xxv. 9, 10; Rev. iii. 18; Prov. xxiii. 23. The contrast between the one pearl found, and the many which he had been seeking, is not to be overlooked. Martha and Mary are illustrations of this point (Luke x. 41, 42). There is but one such pearl, since the truth is one, even as God is one; and the truth possessed brings that unity into the heart of man which sin has destroyed. Only when man has found God does the great Eureka break forth from his lips.[1]

It may be worth while to mention, before closing, the following singular interpretation: the merchant seeking goodly pearls is Christ; the Church of the elect is the pearl of price; to make which his own he parted with all that he had, emptying himself of his divine glory, and taking the form of a servant.

CHAPTER VII.

THE DRAW NET

Matt. xiii. 47-50.

ALTHOUGH at first sight this parable would seem to say exactly the same thing as that of the Tares,[1] yet there is this fundamental difference: that the central truth of that is the *present* intermixture of the good and bad; of this, the *future* separation; of that, that men are not to effect the separation; of this, that the separation will one day be effected by God. That concerns the gradual development,—this, the final consummation of the Church.

Our Lord did not contemplate His visible Church as a perfect communion; but as there was a Ham in the Ark, and a Judas among the twelve, so there should be a Babylon even within the bosom of the spiritual Israel. We may notice what manner of net it is which is here spoken of. It is called a draw net, and the particular kind is specified by the word in the original. On the coast of Cornwall, England, where it is now used, and bears the same name, *seine* or *sean,* it is sometimes half a mile in length. It is leaded below that it may sweep the bottom of the sea, and supported with corks above; and having been carried out so as to inclose a large space of sea, the ends are brought together, and it is drawn upon the beach with all that it contains. This all-embracing nature of the net must not be left out of sight, but contains in fact a prophecy of the wide reach and potent operation of the Gospel (John xi. 52). As the servants told of in Matt. xxii. 10, "gathered together all, as many as they found, both bad and good," so here the fishers take fish of all kinds within the folds of the net; men of all shades of moral character have the Gospel preached to them, and find themselves within the limits of the visible Church.

51

But we read that the net, *when it was full, they drew to shore, and sat down, and gathered the good into vessels, but cast the bad away*. The *sitting down* of the fishers to the task of separation many indicate that it will be done with entire consideration, and without haste. When the number of God's elect is accomplished, then the separation of the precious from the vile shall follow. The "leaving" and "taking," in Matt. xxiv. 40, 41 is most likely to be explained by some such image as this. Probably there, as here, the *taking* is for blessedness, the *leaving* for destruction. The dead or worthless fish are *cast away*. An entire freedom from all evil belongs to the idea of the Church. In this, as in many other passages, the Church is contemplated as a holy inclosure, into which nothing unclean has a right to enter, and from which, if it has by stealth or force effected an entrance, it shall finally be excluded, even as those ceremonially unclean, in witness of this, were obliged to remain for a season without the camp, which was the figure of the true kingdom of God. What the "barn" was at ver. 30, the *vessels* are here; the "many mansions" (John xiv. 2) which the Lord went to prepare for his people. Compare Luke xvi. 9; Heb. xi. 10.

In the familiar occurrence which supplies the groundwork of the parable, the same who carried out the net would naturally be they who would inspect its contents, for the purpose of selecting the good, and casting the worthless away; but it is pushing this circumstances, which is, in fact, the weak side of the comparison, too far, to require that the same should also hold good in the spiritual thing signified. When the Lord interprets the parables, he passes over without a word the beginning of it; and explains only the latter part, where the point and stress of it lay: *So shall it be at the end of the world: the angels shall come forth[2] and sever the wicked from among the just, and shall cast them into the furnace of fire*. We may here find an emphasis in the words *coming forth*. The angels have been hidden ever since the first constitution of the Church.

But then, at that great epoch of the kingdom, they shall again "come forth" from before the throne of God, and walk up and down among men, the visible ministers of his judgments.

The moral of this parable is different from that of the Tares. This teaches us that we be not content with being enclosed within the Gospel-net,—that "they are not all Israel who are of Israel," —but that, in the "great house" of the Church, "there are not only vessels of gold and silver, but of wood and earth, and some to honor and some to dishonor;" that each of us therefore seek to be "a vessel unto honor, sanctified and meet for the master's use" (2 Tim. ii. 20, 21), since in the midst of all confusions, "the Lord knoweth them that are his," and will one day bring all confusion to an end, separating forever the precious from the vile.

The seven parables related in this chapter, were (as many have supposed) in a certain sense prophetical, for they foretold things that were to come to pass;[3] only it was not the Lord's main purpose to acquaint his servants with the future destinies of his Church, but rather to give them practical rules and warnings for their conduct. So, too, they all have a certain unity, succeeding one another in natural order; thus, in the Sower, are set forth the causes of the failures and success which the word of the Gospel meets, when preached in the world. In the Tares, the obstacles to the *internal* development of Christ's kingdom are declared, and are traced up to their true author, with a warning against unwarranted human intervention. The Mustard Seed and the Leaven declare the victorious might— the first the outward, the second the inward might, of that kingdom. As these two are objective and general, so the two which follow are subjective and individual, declaring the relation of the kingdom to every man, and how those who have discovered its supreme worth will be willing to renounce all things for its sake. This last parable declares how that entire separation from evil, which in the second we saw that men might be tempted to anticipate by improper methods, shall yet come to pass; and looking forward to which, each is to strive that he may so use his present means of grace that he may be found among those who shall be the Lord's.

CHAPTER VIII.

THE UNMERCIFUL SERVANT

Matt. xviii. 23-35.

CHRYSOSTOM observes, that when Peter (v. 21) instanced seven as the number of times that an offending brother should be forgiven,[1] he thought certainly he was doing some great thing,—these seven being four times more than the Jewish masters enjoined. They grounded the duty of forgiving no oftener than three times on Amos i. 3 and ii. 6; also Job xxxiii. 29, 30 (see the marginal translation). There was in Peter's mind a consciousness of the new law of love,[2] which Christ had brought into the world,—though an obscure one, since he supposed it possible that love could ever be overcome by hate. But there was a fundamental error in the question itself, for in proposing a limit to our forgiveness, there was implied the notion, that a man in forgiving gave up a right which he might, under certain circumstances, exercise. The purpose of this parable is to make clear that when God calls on a member of His kingdom to forgive, He does not call on him to renounce a right, but that he has now no right to exercise in the matter; asking for and accepting forgiveness, he has implicitly pledged himself to show it.

Therefore, that you may understand the better what I say, is the kingdom of heaven likened unto a certain king, which would take account of his servants. This is the first of the parables in which God appears in His character of King. We are the servants. It is plain this is not the *final* reckoning, but such as is mentioned in Luke xvi. 2. To this He brings us by the preaching of the law — by the setting of our sins before our face — by leading us into adversities; He takes account with us, when through one means or another He brings our careless

55

security to an utter end. Compare 2 Sam. xii.; the Ninevites; the Jews, through John the Baptist.

*And when he had begun to reckon, one was brought unto him, which owed him ten thousand talents.*3 He had only *begun to reckon;* this was perhaps the first into whose accounts he looked. This one *was brought unto him;* he never would have come of himself; he would have made that ten into twenty thousand, for the secure sinner goes on treasuring up (Rom. ii. 5) an even mightier sum, to be one day required of him. In all probability, from the immensity of the debt, this man was one to whom some chief post of honor and dignity in the kingdom had been committed, — a satrap who should have remitted the revenues of his province to the royal treasury.

The sale of the debtor's wife and children — for the king commanded them to be sold with him — rested upon the theory that they were a part of his property.4 By the selling here may be indicated God's alienation of the wicked from Himself, and their everlasting destruction from the presence of the Lord, and the glory of His power. Compare Ps. xliv. 12.

The servant, hearing the dreadful doom, *fell down and worshipped him* — prostrated himself on the ground, kissing his feet and knees. This servant *worshipped* the king; the other servant only *besought* his fellow-servant. His words, *Lord, have patience with me, and I will pay thee all,* show the extreme fear of the moment, which made him ready to promise impossible things, even mountains of gold, if he might but be delivered from the present danger. The sinner using such words, shows that he expects the future obedience can make up for past disobedience. At the earnestness of his prayer, *the Lord of that servant was moved with compassion, and loosed him, and foregave him the debt.* The severity of God, having brought the sinner to a sense of his sin, reappears (for it has been only love in disguise) as grace again. His lord *forgave him the debt,* and thus this very reckoning, which threatened ruin, might have been the greatest mercy of all. God will forgive; but He will have the sinner to know what and how much he is forgiven. But too soon this mercy was forgotten, for going out from the presence of his lord, he found *one of his fellow-servants, who owed him a hundred pence.* That word, *going out,* is one of the key-words of the parable. It is because we "go out" of the presence of our God, because we do not *abide* there, that we are ever in danger of acting as this servant.[5] By the servant's going out is expressed the sinner's forgetfulness of the benefits received from God. The term *fellow-servant* does not imply an equality of rank between the two, but only that they were both servants to a common lord; and the small sum of his debt is mentioned, to show how little man can offend against his brother, compared with the amount in which every man has offended against his God.[6]

He laid hands on him, and took him by the throat, saying, Pay me that thou owest. His fellow-servant fell down at his feet, and besought him, using exactly the same words which he himself had used, and using, had found mercy; but he was inexorable; — he *went,* dragging the debtor with him, till he could deliver him to the jailer. The man who knows not his own guilt is ever ready to exclaim with David, "The man that hath done this thing shall surely die;" while, on the contrary, it is they that are spiritual to whom Paul commits the restoring of an offending brother (Gal. vi. 1). It is *just* in man to be humane, — to be humane is human; none but the altogether righteous may press his utmost rights, and this no man is.

When his fellow-servants saw what was done, they were very sorry. They were *sorry;* their lord was wroth. This distinction is not accidental. In man, the sense of his own guilt, the deep consciousness that whatever sin he sees ripen in another, exists in its germ in his own heart, will ever cause him to feel sorrow when the spectacle of moral evil is brought before his eyes; but in God, the pure hatred of sin — His love of holiness on its negative side — finds place. Being sorry, *they came and told their lord all that was done;* even as the righteous complain to God, and mourn in their prayer over the oppressions wrought in their sight, and which they are powerless to redress. The king summons the unthankful servant into his presence, and uses severe words, which in view of the great debt he had not used, *O thou wicked servant; I forgave thee all that debt, because thou desiredst me: shouldst not thou also have had compassion on thy fellow-servant, even as I had pity on thee?* The guilt laid to his charge is, not that needing mercy he refused to show it, but that *having received* mercy, he remains unmerciful still; a most important difference! — so that they who like him are hard and cruel, do not thereby bear witness that they have received no mercy; on the contrary, their offence is, that having received an infinite mercy, they remain unmerciful yet. The great mercy for the world, that Christ has put away sin, stands firm, whether we allow it to have a purifying influence on our hearts or not.

And his lord was wroth, and delivered him to the tormentors, according to the warning in James ii. 13. *The tormentors* are not merely the keepers of the prison; but those who shall make the life of the prisoner bitter to him; even as there are *tormentors* in the world of woe — fellow-sinners and evil angels. It is strange that the king finally delivers up the offender, not for cruelty, but for the very debt which would appear to have been entirely remitted to him. The question is here involved, Do sins once forgiven, return on the sinner through his after offences? But do not the difficulties of such a question arise from our viewing the forgiveness of sins in too formal a way; — from our suffering the early circumstances of the remission of a debt, to embarrass the heavenly truth, instead of regarding them as helps, and often weak ones, for the setting forth of that truth? A state of nature is itself a state of condemnation. If, then, laying aside the contemplation of a man's sins as a formal debt, which must either be forgiven him or not, we contemplate the life out of Christ as a state of wrath, and the life in Christ as a state of grace, we can better understand how a man's sins may return upon him; that is, he sinning anew falls back into the darkness out of which he had been delivered, and all that he has done of former evil, adds to the darkness (John v. 14). He that is to partake of the final salvation must abide in Christ, else he will be "cast forth as a branch and withered." This is the condition belonging to the very essence of salvation itself. 1 John i. 7 is an interesting parallel.

The Romish theologians find an argument for purgatory in the words, *till he should pay all that was due,* as also in Matt. v. 26. But it seems plainly a proverbial expression; for since man could never acquit the slightest portion of the debt which he owes to God, the putting of such a condition was the strongest possible way of expressing the eternal duration of his punishment. The Lord concludes with an earnest warning: *So likewise shall my heavenly Father do also unto you, if ye from your hearts forgive not every one his brother their trespasses.* So, — with the same rigor; such treasures of wrath, as well as such treasures of grace, are with Him. We may observe that, according to Scripture views, the Christian stands in a middle point, between a mercy received and a mercy yet needed. Sometimes the first is used as an argument for showing mercy — "forgiving one another, as Christ forgave you" (Col. iii. 13; Eph. iv. 32) ; sometimes the last, "Blessed are the merciful, for they shall obtain mercy" (Matt. v. 7; Luke vi. 37; James v. 9).

CHAPTER IX.

THE LABORERS IN THE VINEYARD

Matt. xx. 1-16.

THIS parable stands in the closest connection with the four last verses of the preceeding chapter, and can only be rightly understood by their help. On the right tracing of this connection, and the showing how the parable grew out of, and was in fact an answer to, Peter's question, "What shall we have?" the success of the exposition will mainly depend. Numerous difficulties beset the explanation. There is first the difficulty of bringing the parable into harmony with the saying by which it is introduced and concluded, and which it is plainly intended to illustrate; secondly, there is the moral difficulty, viz., how can one who is a member of the kingdom of God grudge in his heart the favors shown to other members of that kingdom? or, if it is denied that these murmurers are members of the kingdom, how can we reconcile the fact of their having labored all day in the vineyard, and finally carrying away their own reward? And lastly, there is the difficulty of deciding what is the particular point of the parable, what is its main doctrine.

There have been various interpretations of this parable. One of the best is that which makes it a warning and a prophecy of the causes which would lead to the rejection of the Jews, the first called into the vineyard of the Lord; — these causes being mainly their proud appreciation of themselves, and their dislike at seeing the Gentiles admitted at once to equal privileges with themselves in the kingdom of God. An agreement or covenant being made with those first hired, and none with those subsequently engaged, has seemed a confirmation of this view. It *was* notably fulfilled in the Jews; but its application is universal and not particular; this fulfilment was only one out of many.

61

Had this been exclusively, or even primarily our Lord's meaning, we should expect to hear of but two bands of laborers, the first hired and the last; all those who come between would only serve to confuse the image.

Better, then, to say that the parable is directed against a wrong spirit of mind, which indeed was notably manifested in the Jews, but which all men in possession of spiritual privileges are here warned against; while the immediate occasion from which the parable arose, was not one in which they (the Jews) were involved. The warning was not primarily addressed to them, but to the Apostles, and the earliest called to labor in the Lord's vineyard, — *the first,* both in time, and the amount of toil and suffering they would have to undergo. They had seen the rich young man (xix. 22) go away, unable to abide the proof by which the Lord had revealed to him how strongly he was yet holden to the things of the world. Peter, as their spokesman, would fain know what *their* reward would be who had done this very thing from which he had shrunk, and had forsaken all for the Gospel's sake (ver. 27). The Lord answers first and fully in the verses following (vers. 28, 29). But the question, "What shall we have?" was not a right one; there was a tendency to bring their obedience to a calculation of so much work, so much reward. There was also lurking a certain self-complacency in the speech, a comparison for self-exaltation with others; *they* had not shrunk from the command to forsake all, as the young man had. Unless the answer which the Lord gave had been accompanied with the warning of the parable, it would but have served as fuel to the fire. "Not of works, lest any man should boast;" this was the truth which He would now by the parable enforce; and if nothing of works but all of grace for all, then no claim as of right upon the part of any. In short, the spirit of the hireling spoke in that question, and it is against this spirit that the parable is directed, which might be entitled, On the nature of rewards in the kingdom of God, —

the whole finding a most instructive commentary in Rom. iv. 1-4, which passage supplies a parallel with the present.

As far as it is addressed to all true believers, the parable is rather a warning against what might be, than a prophecy of what would be. For we cannot imagine him who dwells in love as allowing himself in envious thoughts against any of his brethren,[1] because, though they have entered later on the service of God, they will yet be sharers with him of the same heavenly reward. Least of all, can we imagine him to allow such hateful feelings actually to take shape, or as justifying them to himself or to God, like the spokesman among the murmurers here. The lesson taught is, that those who seem chiefest in labor, yet, if they forget that the reward is of grace, and not of works, may *altogether lose* the things which they have wrought; and those who seem last, may, by keeping their humility, be acknowledged first in the day of God.

The kingdom of heaven is like unto a man that is an householder, which went out early in the morning to hire laborers into his vineyard. This is ever true in the spiritual world, that God seeks His laborers, and not they Him (John xv. 16) ; but, as in the natural world a call implies no force, but is something which may be obeyed or refused, so also is it in the spiritual world. The agreement made by these first hired laborers, was exactly the one Peter wished to make, "What shall we have?" — while those subsequently engaged went in a simpler spirit, trusting that whatever was right would be given to them. Thus we see on the one side early indications of that wrong spirit which comes to a head in ver. 11, 12; on the other side we have the true spirit of humble waiting upon the Lord, in full assurance that He will give far more than we can deserve.

At nine in the morning, at mid-day, and at three in the afternoon,[2] he again went into the market-place, and those who were disengaged, he employed. *And about the eleventh hour, he went out and found others standing idle, and saith unto them, Why*

stand ye here all the day idle? All actvity out of Christ is in
His sight a standing idle. *They say unto him, Because no man
hath hired us.* It can only be when the kingdom of God is first
set up in a land, that sinful men with full truth can answer in
these words. The excuse which these laborers plead, appertains
not to them who, growing up within the Church, have despised
nearly to the last God's repeated biddings to go work in His
vineyard. Still one would not deny that there is such a thing
even in the Christian Church as men being called — or, to speak
more correctly, — as men obeying the call long before given,
and entering on God's service, at the third, or ninth, or even the
eleventh hour; who, truly repenting of their past unprofitable-
ness, may find their work graciously accepted now, and may
share hereafter in the full rewards of the kingdom.[3]

*So when even was come, the lord of the vineyard saith unto
his steward, Call the laborers, and give them their hire, beginning
from the last unto the first.* The laborers are called together; the
last hired, those who came in without any agreement made,
receive a full penny.[4] Here is encouragement for those who have
delayed to enter on God's service till late in their lives, to work
heartily, and with their might. But those who were first hired
*murmured against the good man of the house, saying, These last
have wrought but one hour, and thou hast made them equal unto
us, which have borne the burden and heat of the day.* Here the
perplexing dilemma meets us: If these are of God's faithful
people, how can they murmur against Him, and grudge against
their fellows? or if they are not of His people, how can they
at last carry away the penny, the reward of eternal life? But
there is here rather a teaching by contraries; "Since you cannot
imagine such a hateful spirit finding place in the perfected kingdom of God, check its beginnings — check all inclination to took
grudgingly at your brethren, who, having in time past grievously
departed from God, have now found a place beside yourselves
in His kingdom — check all inclination to pride yourselves on

your own doings, as though they gave you a claim of right upon God, instead of receiving all from the free mercy of God."

The penny given to all, though *objectively* the same, *subjectively* is very different; it is, in fact, to every one exactly what he will make it.5 The Lord says, "I am thy exceeding great reward," and He has no other reward to impart to any but this, namely, Himself. To see Him as He is, this is the reward which He has for all His people, the penny unto all. But what these murmuring laborers desire, is not to have *much,* but to have *more* than others; they did not wish to grow together with the whole body of Christ, but to get before their brethren, and the penny, because common to all, did not seem enough — while it was in fact to each what he would make it. For since only like can know like, all advances made here in humility, in holiness, in love, are a polishing of the mirror that it may reflect more distinctly the Divine image, a purging of the eye that it may see more clearly the Divine glory. On the contrary, all self-righteousness and sin of every kind, whether it stop short with impairing or end by altogether destroying the capacities for receiving from God, is in its degree a staining of the mirror, a darkening of the eye.

But he answered one of them, probably him who was loudest and foremost, *and said, Friend, I do thee no wrong: didst thou not agree with me for a penny?* He justifies his manner of dealing with them, as well as his sovereign right in his own things. They had put their claim on the footing of right, and on that footing they are answered, *Take that thine is, and go thy way;* and again, *Is thine eye evil because I am good?* so long as I am just to you, may I not be good and liberal to them?6 Envy is ever spoken of as finding its expression in the eye (Deut. xv. 9; 1 Sam. xviii. 9 — "Saul *eyed* David"). The solution of the difficulty that these complainers should get their reward is, that according to human relations, on which the parable is founded, and to which it must adapt itself, it would not have been consistent with equity to have made them forfeit their hire, notwithstanding the bad feeling which they displayed. But the words which follow, *So the last shall be first, and the first last,* sufficiently indicate that with God an absolute forfeiture might follow, nay, must follow, where this grudging, unloving spirit has come to its full head.

Many have been troubled to bring these last words (*"So the last . . .*) into agreement with the parable; for in it first and last seem all put on the same footing, while here a complete change of place is asserted. Some have sought an explanation in the fact that the last hired are the first in order of payment; but this to too trifling an advantage. What has been already observed may furnish a sufficient answer; the saying is necessary to complete the moral — to express that which the parable did not and could not express, viz., the *entire* forfeiture which would follow on the indulgence of such a temper as that here displayed.

The words which follow, *Many be called, but few chosen,* are difficult, on account of the position which they occupy. Olshausen makes the *called* and the *chosen* alike partakers of final salvation, but holds that by these terms are signified different standings of men in the kingdom of God. The easiest interpretation seems to be, — Many are called to work in God's vineyard, but few retain that humility, that utter denial of any claim as of right on their own part, which will allow them in the end to be partakers of His reward. — In the reward[7] there is a certain retrospect to the work done, but no proportion between them, except such as may have been established by the free appointment of the Giver. "He is faithful that promised;" this, and not any other thing, must remain always the ground of all expectations and hopes; and what these are to be and what they are not to be, it is the main purpose of this parable to declare.

CHAPTER X.

THE TWO SONS

Matt. xxi. 28-32.

IN THE 23rd verse of this chapter we see that our Lord was asked a question by His adversaries, they hoping to find accusation against Him. Now He becomes the assailing party, and begins that series of parables, in which, as in a glass, they might see themselves. Yet they are not spoken in words of defiance, but of earnest love — if possibly He might save them from the fearful sin they were about to commit.

But what think ye? — A certain man had two sons. Under the image of two sons are ranged almost all with whom our Lord came in contact. Of one of these classes the Pharisees were specimens, though all are included who have sought a righteousness through the law. In the second class are contained all who have openly transgressed the laws of God. The condition of these first is preferable, provided they give place to the righteousness of faith when that appears. But if their righteousness is cold and proud, and imagines that it wants nothing, then far better off is the sinner who has his eyes opened to perceive his misery and guilt, even though it should have been by grievous transgressions. The same lesson is taught us in all Scripture — that there is no such fault as counting we have no fault. Compare Rom. vii. 7-9; Luke xviii. 10-14.

And he came to the first and said, Son, go work to-day in my vineyard. This was the general summons made both by the natural law in the conscience, and also by the revealed law which Moses gave, to bring forth fruit unto God. The son first bidden *said, I will not.* He does not say, "I pray thee, have me excused," but flatly refuses; he is the representative of careless, reckless sinners. *And he came to the second and said likewise; and he answered and said, I go, sir.* The Scribes and Pharisees professed zeal for the law, but their profession was like the second son's promised obedience; for when the time arrived when it was necessary to be on one side or the other, when John the Baptist came to them and summoned them to earnest repentance, their real unrighteousness was declared; professing willingness to go, they yet *went not.* On the other hand, many of those who had been openly profane, were baptized, confessing their sins, and like the son who at first refused to do his father's bidding, *repented and went.*

The Lord then asks, *Whether of the twain did the will of his father?* They are obliged to reply, *The first,* of course, in comparison with the other. The Lord immediately makes the application, *Verily I say unto you, that the publicans and harlots go into the kingdom of God before you.* In the words, *go before you,* or take the lead of you, he would indicate that the door of hope was yet open; the others had indeed preceded them, but they might still follow, if they would. Some interpreters lay an emphasis on the words, *in the way of righteousness,* as though Christ would say, "The Baptist came, a pattern of that very righteousness of the law, in which you profess to exercise yourselves. He did not come, calling to the new life of the Gospel, of which I am the pattern; he did not come, seeking to put new wine into old bottles; but he came, fulfilling that idea of righteousness which you pretended to have set before yourselves, which consisted in separation from sinners; and yet you rejected him, and when ye had seen the fruits of his ministry in the conversion of sinners, repented not, that ye might believe him."

This parable does not primarily apply to the Jews and Gentiles, but must be referred rather to the two bodies within the bosom of the Jewish people: — it is not said, the Gentiles enter heaven before you, but the publicans and harlots.

CHAPTER XI.

THE WICKED HUSBANDMEN

Matt. xxi. 33-44; Mark xii. 1-12; Luke xx. 9-18.

MATTHEW and Mark relate this parable as addressed to the Pharisees, while, according to St. Luke, it was addressed to the people. But this is explained by the account itself, Luke mentioning the chief priests and scribes (ver. 19), in such a way as to show that they were present as listeners.

The image of the kingdom of God as a vine-stock, or as a vineyard,[1] runs through the whole Old Testament (Ps. lxxx. 8-16; Isa. v. 1-7; xxvii. 1-7; Jer. ii. 21). No property was considered to yield so large a return, and none required such unceasing care. Our Lord compares Himself to the vine as the noblest of earthly plants (John xv. 1), and in prophecy had been compared to it long before (Gen. xlix. 11). We cannot interpret the vineyard here, as the Jewish Church, since it is said to be taken away from the Jews, and given to another nation; we must rather understand by it the kingdom of God in its idea, which idea Jew and Gentile have been successively placed in conditions to realize.

The householder not only possessed this vineyard; he had himself *planted* it. The planting of this spiritual vineyard found place under Moses and Joshua, in the establishment of the Jewish polity in the land of Canaan (Deut. xxxii. 12-14; Ezek. xvi. 9-14; Neh. ix. 23-25). By the hedging of it round about, we may understand their circumscription through the law, the Jews thus becoming a people dwelling alone, and not reckoned among the nations (Num. xiii. 9). In keeping distinct the line of separation between themselves and the idolatrous nations, lay their security that they should enjoy the protection of God

69

(Zech. ii. 5, Isai. xxvi). Outwardly also, Judea was hedged about through its geographical position, between the Jordan and the two lakes, the desert and Idumea, the sea and Anti-Libanus. The wine-press and the tower would both be necessary to a vineyard. The tower was not merely for ornament, a kiosk, but a place of shelter for the watchmen, who should protect the fruits. The wine-press was often made by digging out the earth, and lining it with masonry. In the press above, the grapes were placed, and were commonly crushed out by the feet of men (Judg. ix. 27; Isa. lxiii. 3). A closely-grated hole at the bottom of the press permitted the juice to pass through into the vat. Nothing more is probably meant by these arrangements than that God provided His people with all things necessary for life and godliness.[2]

He let it out to husbandmen. The vineyard itself will signify the great body of the people, who were to be taught, to the end that they might bring forth fruits of righteousness; and the husbandmen may be compared to the priests and Levites to whose charge this vineyard was given; their solemn commission is recognized in such passages as Mal. ii. 7; Ezek. xxxiv. 2. Every thing implies that they had entered into covenant with the proprietor, even as the Jewish people made a covenant with God at Horeb. The householder then *went into a far country, for a long while.* At Sinai, and in the miracles which accompanied the deliverance from Egypt, the Lord may be said to have openly manifested Himself to Israel, and then to have withdrawn Himself for a while, not speaking to the people again face to face (Deut. xxxiv. 10-12), but waiting in patience to see what manner of works the people under the teaching of their spiritual guides would bring forth.

And when the time of the fruit drew near, he sent his servants to the husbandmen that they might receive the fruits of it. These servants are to be explained as meaning the prophets who *were sent,* being raised up at particular times, having particular missions — their power lying in their mission. They were sent to receive *of the fruit of the vineyard,* the householder's share of the produce — the rent being paid in a fixed proportion of the fruits. Olshausen says: "These fruits which are demanded, are not to be explained as particular works, but rather as the repentance, and inward longing after true righteousness, which the law was unable to bring about. The servants therefore are those who seek for these spiritual needs, that they may link to them the promises concerning a coming Redeemer."

When the first servant came, they *beat him, and sent him away empty;* the next they beat, and *entreated him shamefully.* The third they wounded and cast out of the vineyard with violence. In St. Luke's narrative the last and worst outrage is reserved for the son himself, but if we may trust Jewish tradition, Jeremiah was stoned by the exiles in Egypt, Isaiah was sawn asunder by king Manasseh; and see 2 Kings, vi. 31; 2 Chron. xxiv. 20, 21; xxxvi. 16; Acts vii. 52; and the whole passage finds a parallel in Hebrew xi. 36. The patience of the householder under these extraordinary provocations is wonderful; and it is thus brought out that it may set forth the yet more wonderful long-suffering of God; Jer. xliv. 4. The whole confession made by the Levites in Neh. ix., is an admirable commentary on this parable.

But last of all he sent unto them his son,[3] *his well-beloved, saying, They will reverence my son* (Heb. i. 1). This was the last and crowning effort of Divine mercy, after which, on the one side, all the resources even of heavenly love are exhausted, on the other the measure of sins is perfectly filled up. Christ was a Son in the highest sense of the word (Heb. iii. 5, 6). *But when the husbandmen saw the son, they said among themselves, This is the heir;*[4] *come, let us kill him, and let us seize on his inheritance.* Compare John xi. 47-53; and the counsels of Joseph's brethren against him (Gen. xxxvii. 19). As they, thinking to defeat the purpose of God, helped to bring it to pass, so the Jewish rulers were the instruments to fulfil that purpose

of God concerning Christ which they meant to bring to nothing
(Acts iii. 18; iv. 27, 28). *This is the heir;* he to whom the
inheritance will in due time descend. The husbandmen say,
Come, let us kill him; not that the Pharisees ever said such a
thing in so many words; but they desired the inheritance, they
desired that what God had intended should only be temporary,
enduring till the times of reformation, should be made permanent, — and this because they had privileges under the imperfect system which would cease when the more perfect scheme
was brought in, or rather which would be transformed into higher
privileges for which they had no care. *And they caught him and
cast him out of the vineyard, and slew him.* By this we are reminded of Him who "suffered without the gate" (Heb. xiii. 12,
13; John xix. 17). By that, as by the exclusion from the camp,
was signified the cutting off from the people of God, and from
all share in their blessings. Having thus prophesied of their
conduct[5] to the Jewish rulers, Christ asks, *When the lord therefore of the vineyard cometh, what will he do unto those husbandmen?* We see how the successive generations, who for so many
centuries had been filling up the measure of the iniquity of Israel,
are considered, through this parable, as but one body of husbandmen. God's truth is opposed to that shallowness which would
make such a word as "nation" a dead abstraction. God will deal
with nations, as in fact *bodies,* and not as being merely convenient terms to express certain aggregations of individuals.[6]
There is no injustice in this; for while there is a life of the
whole, there is a life of each part, so that even if we should
belong to a nation in that of its generations which is chastised
for its own and its fathers' iniquities, yet it remains always possible for each individual by faith and repentance to withdraw himself from that which really constitutes the calamity, — the wrath
of God.

In the question itself, *What will he do unto those husbandmen?* Christ makes the same appeal to his hearers as Isaiah had

done (v. 3), compelling them to condemn themselves out of their own mouths. Vitringa observes: "God condemns no one who is not condemned by his own conscience. For God has in every man His judgment-seat, and *by man* He judges concerning man." It may be, from the answer of the Pharisees, *He will miserably destroy those wicked men, and will let out his vineyard unto other husbandmen,* that they did not see the point of the parable, or perhaps it may be, as Olshausen says, that they pretended not to see its drift, and that therefore Christ spoke more plainly in ver. 42-44: *Therefore I say unto you, The kingdom of God shall be taken from you, and given to a nation bringing forth the fruits thereof.* Then at length, Christ and His adversaries stood face to face. The *God forbid* uttered by the people (Luke xx. 16), gives evidence that *they* had understood the parable, even before its plain interpretation at the last.

Our Lord then quotes a prophecy from the Old Testament, proving that such a turn of things had been contemplated long before in the counsels of God. "Did ye never read in the Scriptures, The stone which the builders rejected, the same is become the head of the corner?" The Psalm (cxviii.) from which it is taken, was recognized by the Jews as applicable to the Messiah. The reason why He leaves for a moment the image of the vineyard, is because of its inadequacy to set forth one important part of the truth, that the malice of the Pharisees should not defeat the purpose of God, — that the Son should yet be Heir. *This* is distinctly declared by the repected stone becoming the head of the corner, on which the builders stumbled and fell, and were broken, and which, if they set themselves against it to the end, would fall upon them, and crush and destroy them utterly. *They* fall on the stone, who are offended at Christ in His low estate (Isaiah viii. 14; Luke ii. 34) ; of this sin His hearers were already guilty. He warns them against a worse sin which they were on the point of committing, and which would be followed by a heavier punishment; they on whom the stone falls, are they who deliberately set themselves in opposition against the Lord — knowing who He is. They shall not merely fall and be broken, for one might, although suffering some harm, recover himself, — but on them the stone shall fall and grind them to powder.

All three Evangelists notice the exasperation of the chief priests and scribes, when they perceive that the parable was spoken against *them;* had they not feared the people, they would have laid violent hands on Him at once.

CHAPTER XII.

THE MARRIAGE OF THE KING'S SON

Matt. xxii. 1-14.

THIS parable, and that which is found at Luke xiv. 16, are not to be confounded with one another. It is plain that they were spoken on different occasions, — that at a meal, this in the temple, and that, too, at a much earlier period of our Lord's ministry than this. Then the hostility of the Pharisees had not yet declared itself;[1] but now they had come to the formal determination of making away with Christ by violent means. In that, the contemptuous guests are merely excluded from the festival,— in this, their city is burned up and themselves destroyed. Their increased guilt is set forth in this one, by the fact of its being a king who makes the festival, and a festival in honor of his son's marriage; by which fact is brought out the relation of the Jews to Jesus, the personal theocratic king, and in every way the guilt involved in their rejection of Him is heightened. Again, in the parable recorded by St. Luke, nothing more is threatened than that God would turn from the priests and Pharisees to another portion of the same nation, the publicans and harlots, — with only a slight intimation of the call of the Gentiles; while here it is threatened that the kingdom of God shall be wholly taken from the Jewish people, and given to the Gentiles.

In the present parable, as compared with the last one, we see how the Lord is revealing Himself in ever clearer light, as the central person of the kingdom. There He was indeed the son; but here His race is royal (Ps. lxxii. 1). That last was a parable of the Old Testament history; even Christ appears there rather as the last of the line of prophets and teachers, than as the founder of a new kingdom. In that, a parable of the law; in this, a parable of grace, God appears as giving something to them.

75

The two favorite images under which the prophets set forth the blessings of the new covenant, — that of a festival (Isai. xxv. 6; lxv. 13), and that of a marriage (Isai. lxi. 10; lxii. 5; Hos. ii. 19, etc.), are united in the marriage festival here.[2] There appears, indeed, an inconvenience in the fact that the members of the Church are at once the guests invited to the feast, and in their collective capacity constitute the bride at whose espousals the feast is given; but in the progress of the narrative the circumstances of the marriage altogether fall into the background, and the different conduct of the invited guests becomes the prominent feature. This parable has its groundwork in the Old Testament (Exod. xxiv. 11; Zeph. i. 7, 8), and it entered into the circle of Jewish expectations that the Messiah's kingdom should be ushered in by a glorious festival. Our Lord Himself (Luke xxii. 18, 30) uses this image. It is true that the marriage is spoken of there, and at Rev. xix. 7, as not taking place till the end of the present age, while here the Lord speaks of it as present; but we must keep in mind how distinct were the espousals and the actual marriage in the East, and contemplate His first coming as the time of His espousals, while not till His second coming will He lead home His bride.

At a fitting time the king *sent forth his servants to call them that were bidden to the wedding.* This second invitation, or rather admonishment, is quite according to Eastern manners (Esth. v. 8; vi. 14). Modern travellers testify that the same custom still prevails. When Christ says, *to call them that were bidden,* He would have His hearers understand, that there was nothing sudden in the coming in of His kingdom. The invitation first went forth at the constitution of the Jewish nation as God's elect people, and ran through all their history, being taken up and repeated by each succeeding prophet. Yet they never did more than thus bid the guests, for they only spoke of good things to come. The actual calling of "them that were bidden" did not pertain to them. John the Baptist was the first in whose

time the kingdom was actually present, the wedding-feast prepared, the king and the king's son manifested, and the long-
invited guests summoned. By the first band of servants, I
understand John and the Apostles in their first mission — that
which they accomplished during the lifetime of our Lord. His
own share in summoning the guests unto Himself, "Come unto
me," is naturally kept out of sight in the parable, as it would
have disturbed the proprieties of the characters represented. We
see here that there was no actual maltreatment of these first
messengers, — nor was there at the first against the Lord, nor
against the Apostles during His lifetime. (The death of John
cannot be urged here; for Herod was an Edomite, and therefore
not an invited guest; and moreover it was for preaching the law,
not the Gospel, that he died.) It was simply *they would not
come. Ye will not* come to me, etc.

Again he sent forth other servants. Here is described that
renewed invitation to the Jews, which was made subsequent to the
Crucifixion. There need be no perplexity in the words *"other*
servants;" for there *were* many others besides the Apostles, such
as Stephen, Paul, Barnabas. Those, too, who were the same,
went forth as new men, full of the Holy Ghost, not preaching
generally a kingdom of God, but "Jesus and the resurrection;"
declaring that all things were ready — that all the obstacles
reared up by man's sin, were removed by God's grace (Acts ii.
38, 39; iii. 19-26) ; that in that very blood, which had been
impiously shed, there was forgiveness of all sins. And let us
notice that the king, instead of threatening or rebuking, told
his servants only to press the message with greater urgency. *Tell
them which are bidden,* so tell them that they cannot mistake,
that *all things are ready. (My oxen and my fatlings are killed.*
This would be a sign of the immediate nearness of the feast.
Chardin: In the morning the mutton and lamb are killed, which
are to be eaten in the evening.) It was exactly thus with the
Apostles; thus Peter (Acts iii. 17), — "I wot that through

ignorance ye did it;" — how did they refuse to dwell upon the past sin, urging rather the present grace!

But the guests *made light of it, and went their ways, one to his farm, another to his merchandise.* Nor is this the worst; *The remnant took his servants, and entreated them spitefully, and slew them.* So there are ever in the world two kinds of despisers of the Gospel of God; some who may say, "I pray thee have me excused," — others in whom it excites feelings of positve enmity. Those in the first class are again subdivided; for they "went their ways, one to his farm, another to his merchandise." The question naturally arises, Did the Lord intend a distinction? The dangers of *having* ("one to his farm or estate"), and of *getting* ("another to his merchandise"), though cognate, are yet not at all the same.[3] There are those who are full, and there are those who are hoping to be full, of this world; in neither has the divine hunger ever been awakened in the soul.

The remnant took his servants, and entreated them spitefully, and slew them. The oppositions to the Gospel are not merely natural, they are also devilish. There are other evils in the heart besides worldliness, stirred up by it. It wounds men's pride, affronts their self-righteousness, and they visit on the bringers of it the hate they bear to itself. The Acts of the Apostles and later Scriptures bear abundant evidence of the three forms of outrage mentioned here. They *took his servants* (Acts iv. 3; v. 18; viii. 3); they *entreated them spitefully* (Acts v. 40; xiv. 5, 19; xvii. 5; xxi. 30; xxiii. 2); they *slew them* (Acts vii. 58; xii. 3; compare Matt. xxiii. 34). To this part of the parable, 2 Chron. xxx. 1-11 forms an interesting parallel.—But one of the latest cavillers (Strauss) thinks it inconceivable that invited guests should act thus. May we not presume, however, that a deep alienation from their king, with a readiness to rebel against him, existing long before, found its utterance here?[4] The little apparent motive makes their conduct almost monstrous, yet thus fitter to declare the monstrous fact that men should slay the messengers of God's grace, the ambassadors of Christ.

But when the king heard thereof, he was wroth. The insult was intended for him; and as such it was avenged; for he *sent forth his armies,* that is, say some, his avenging angels (Rev. xix. 14), or it may be the hosts of Rome (Dan. ix. 26), which were equally *his armies,* since even ungodly men are men of God's hand, by whom He executes vengeance on other wicked (compare Isai. x. 5, etc.). It may mean both combined, for when God's wrath is to be executed, the visible and the unseen instrumentalities are evermore leagued together. The natural eye sees only one, the spiritual eye sees also the other.[5] The *city of those murderers* can be no other than Jerusalem. It is *their* city, not any longer the city of the great King, who acknowledges it no more for His own. Compare "*Your* house" (Matt. xxiii. 38).

Then (compare Acts xiii. 46) *saith he to his servants, The wedding is ready, but they which were bidden were not worthy.* Their unworthiness consisted in their rejection of the invitation, even as the worthiness of those who did find a place at the festival consisted in their acceptance of the invitation. *Go ye therefore into the highways,[6] and as many as ye shall find, bid to the marriage.* Here the doctrine so hateful to Jewish ears (Acts xxii. 21, 22), the calling of the Gentiles, and that through the Jews' disobedience, is again plainly declared (Rom. xi.; Matt. viii. 10-12). Hereupon the servants *went out into the highways, and gathered together all, as many as they found, both bad and good.* In the spirit of this command, Philip went down to Samaria, and Peter baptized Cornelius and his company. When it is said they gathered in "bad" as well as "good," we are not to see in it an explantion of the fact that one should hereafter be found at the festival without a wedding garment. On the contrary, many were *bad* when invited, who through acceptance of the invitation, passed into the number of *good.*

Neither must the terms be pressed too far, for none (speaking with strict accuracy) are good, till they are incorporated into the body of Christ. Yet, few will deny that there are different degrees of moral life, even before obedience to the call of the Gospel. Cornelius, or those mentioned in Rom. ii. 14, are instances of being *good,* while by *bad* we mean those who to man seem hoplessly gone in moral depravity (see 1 Cor. vi. 9-11). The invitation is accepted by some of both classes; *The wedding was furnished with guests.*

There is still another solemn act of judgment to follow. There is to be a second separation. We have had the judgment on the avowed foe; that on the false friend is yet to find place. But it is not the servants' office here, any more than in the Tares, to make it. *When the king came in to see the guests, he saw there a man which had not on a wedding garment.* Him he addresses, though mildly; for it was yet to be seen whether he could explain his conduct. *Friend, how camest thou in hither, not having a wedding garment?* But, he was *speechless.* It was part of the state of wealthy persons in the East, to have great store of costly dresses laid up (Isa. iii. 6; 2 Kings x. 22). Chardin says, "The expenditure of the king of Persia for presents cannot be credited. The number of dresses which he gives is infinite. His wardrobes are always full of them; they are kept assorted in warehouses." We know, moreover, that costly dresses were often given as honorable presents, marks of especial favor (Gen. xlv. 22; 2 Kings v. 5) ; that they were then, as now, the most customary gifts; and that upon marriage festivals (Est. ii. 18) gifts were distributed with the largest hand. If the gift was one of costly raiment, it would reasonably be expected that it shold be worn at once, to add to the splendor and glory of the festal time—not to say that the rejection of a gift, or the appearance of a slight put upon it, is ever esteemed as a contempt of the giver.[7] But this guest was guilty of a further affront in appearing at the festival in mean and sordid apparel. He did not feel that he had anything to say for himself; *he was speechless,* literally, his mouth was stopped; he stood self-condemned. *Then said the king to the servants, Bind him hand and foot, and take him away, and cast him into outer darkness.* Within the palace was light and joy, but without it was cold and darkness; into this the unworthy guest was to be cast—and there for him, under the sense of his shame, would be "weeping and gnashing of teeth."

But there is much in this latter part of the parable which demands an accurate inquiry. When does the king come in to see, or scrutinize the guests? Not *exclusively* in the day of final judgment, but at every other judgment whereby hypocrites are revealed, or self-deceivers laid bare to themselves or to others, —at every time of trail, which is also in its nature a time of separation, a time when the thoughts of many hearts are disclosed. Some have suggested that by the *singleness* of the guest without a wedding garment, Judas may be pointed out. It certainly is not impossible, but it is hardly probable that any one person is intended, but rather under this one a great multitude, for the *few* said to be chosen in comparison to the *many called* show that there had been a great sifting. Nor is there any difficulty in this view; as the righteous are one, being gathered under their one head, which is Christ, so the wicked are one, being gathered also under their one head, Satan. The mystical Babylon is one city no less than the mystical Jerusalem.

It has been abundantly disputed what particular spiritual grace was lacking in him who was without the wedding garment; the Romanists eagerly asserting it to be charity in opposition to faith.[8] It was righteousness, both in its root of faith and in its flower of charity. According to Paul's image, here peculiarly appropriate, he had not "put on Christ"—in which putting on of Christ both faith and charity are included —the whole adornment of the new and spiritual man. Let us contemplate this guest as a self-righteous man, making and trusting

in a righteousness of his own, instead of believing in a righteousness of Christ's, imputed and imparted,—or let us see in
him a more ordinary sinner, who, with the Christian profession
and privileges, is yet walking after the lusts of the flesh
in sin; he is, in either case, a despiser, counting himself good
enough in himself, in the flesh and not in the spirit, to appear
before God. But a time arrives when every man will discover
that he needs another covering for his soul. Woe unto him who,
like this guest, only discovers it when it is too late to provide
himself with such! It will be the light of God, as it was the
king's word, which will at the last day reveal to him all the
hidden things of his heart, the greater part of which he had
been wilfully ignorant of. He will be speechless; in that day
his mouth will be stopped.

The ministering attendants, different from the servants sent
to invite the guests, can be no other than the angels (Matt.
xiii. 41, 49). They are bidden to *bind him hand and foot.* In
this we may see the sign of the helplessness to which every
striver against God is reduced. *Take him away* refers to the
sinner's exclusion from the Church, now glorious and triumphant
in heaven (Matt. xii. 48; 2 Thess. i. 9). And not only is good
lost, but he bears the presence of evil. They shall *cast him into
outer darkness.* As light is the element of God's kingdom, so
whatever is beyond that kingdom is darkness—the *outer darkness,*
into which all fall back who refuse to walk in the light of
God's truth. This parable terminates with the weighty saying,
Many are called, but few are chosen. In the "called" and not
"chosen," must be included those others also that did not so
much as seem to embrace the invitation, and who suffered in
the destuction of their city. These words do but state a truth
which had long before been finding its fulfilment in the kingdom of God, which, alas! is always accomplishing there. They
were fulfilled in the history of that entire generation which
went out of Egypt—they were all *called,* yet were not in the

end *chosen*, since with most of them God was not well pleased, etc. (1 Cor. x. 1-10; Heb. iii. 7-19). Of the twelve who were sent to see the promised land, only Caleb and Joshua were *chosen*. Of Gideon's army, all were *called*, but only three hundred were *chosen* (Judge. 7).

CHAPTER XIII.

THE TEN VIRGINS[1]

Matt. xxv. 1-13.

THE customs alluded to in this parable still exist in the East. The bridegroom, attended by his friends ("the children of the bride-chamber," Matt. ix. 15; John iii. 29), goes to the house of the bride, and with pomp and gladness brings her to his own home; or if that be too small for the company, to some place provided for the occasion. She is accompanied from her father's house by her young companions (Ps. xlv. 15), while others, the virgins of the parable, meet the procession at some convenient place, and enter with the bridal company into the hall of feasting. As marriages in the East invariably took place, as they still do, in the night, we are told that these virgins *took their lamps.* The number of the virgins is not accidental; it was ruled that wherever there were ten Jews living in one place, there was a congregation, and there a synagogue ought to be built.

The first question is, Who are meant by these virgins? Some argue thus: All are called virgins; all, therefore, belong to Christ. Some, from being unready at the last moment, suffered a long deferring of their blessedness; but none were finally excluded from salvation. This interpretation is generally connected with the doctrine of the thousand years' reign of Christ on the earth, and a first resurrection. There might be some force in this argument, *if others sometimes undertook the office of welcoming the bridegroom, and yet the Lord had chosen to give that appellation to these, and to specify them as virgins.*

Virginity here is the profession of a pure faith, the soul guiltless of apostasy from God. By these virgins, then, we are to understand all who profess to be waiting for the Son of God from heaven, and who do not by their deeds openly deny that hope. They all *took their lamps, and went forth to meet the bridegroom.* But, it is added, *five of them were wise, and five of them were foolish;*[2] so called rather than *good* and *bad,* because even in the foolish some good-will toward the truth is implied in going to meet the bridegroom. See both classes in 2 Pet. i. 5-9. *They that were foolish took their lamps, but took no oil with them; but the wise took oil in their vessels with their lamps.* Here there is a controversy between the Romanists and Reformers,[3] the latter asserting that it was the living principle of faith which was lacking, the Romanists affirming that they had faith, but not having works, it was "dead, being alone." But we may equally contemplate the foolish virgins as those going through a round of external duties, without life; or, on the other hand, as those who, confessing Christ with their lips, are not diligent in acts of humility, charity, etc. It is clear that whatever is merely outward in the Christian profession is the lamp—whatever is inward and spiritual is the oil laid up in the vessels. In either case we must get beyond both works and faith to something higher—the informing Spirit of God, which prompts the works and quickens the faith, and of which oil is ever in Scripture the symbol (Exod. xxx. 22-33; Zech. iv. 2, 12; Heb. i. 9).

The purpose of the parable is, to impress upon the members of the Church their need of vigilance. It adds much to the solemnity of the lesson, that by the foolish virgins are meant, not hypocrites, much less the openly ungodly, but the negligent in prayer, the slothful in work. Nor is it that they have no oil at all; they have some, but not enough. In Matt. xiii. 5, the seed springs up till the sun scorches it; so here, the lamps burn on till their oil is exhausted. In each case there is something more than a merely external profession, conscious that it is only such; there is the Christian life in manifestation, but not fed from deep internal fountains. But *they* are like the wise virgins, who recognize the fact that the Church may not very soon enter into its glory; who foresee that they may have a long life of self-denial, before they shall be called from their labors, before the kingdom shall come unto them; and who consequently feel that they must have principle as well as feeling to carry them on—that their first good impulses will carry them but a little way, unless they be purified and strengthened by a constant supply of the Spirit of God.

When it is said that the bridegroom actually tarried, we may notice it as one of the many hints given by our Lord, of the delay of His return.4 If He had said plainly that He would not come for many centuries, then the first ages of the Church would have been deprived of that powerful motive to holiness and diligence supplied to each generation of the faithful by the possibility of the Lord's return in their time. Besides, prophecy is no fatalism, and it was always open to every age by faith and prayer to *hasten* that coming (2 Pet. iii. 12).

The bridegroom tarrying, the virgins *all slumbered and slept.*5 By the fact of *all* sleeping, some have understood a certain unreadiness that will be found in the whole Church—though, with a portion, this unreadiness will be easily removed, while that of others will be beyond remedy. But Augustine and nearly all the ancient interpreters make it the sleep of death. Perhaps by the sleeping is meant nothing more than that all, having done every thing which they thought needful in order to meet the bridegroom as they would wish, calmly and securely awaited his coming. The fact that the foolish virgins fell asleep, and only awoke at the cry of the advancing company, gives an easy explanation of their utter destitution of oil at the moment of their greatest need. And had the wise virgins been watching while the others slept, it would have seemed like a lack of love not to have warned their companions of the increasing dimness with which their lamps were burning, while yet help was possible.

It was not until midnight that *there was a cry made, Behold the bridegroom cometh; go ye out to meet him;*—this cry was made either by part of the retinue, or by the applauding multitude. As to its spiritual signification, most are agreed to find an allusion to "the voice of the Archangel and the trump of God" (1 Thess. iv. 16). Some, however, explain the cry as coming from those watchers in the Church by whom the signs of the times have been observed, and who would proclaim aloud the near advent of the Heavenly Bridegroom, leading home the triumphant Church, and looking to be met by the members of His Church yet militant. It was a current opinion among the Jews, that the Messiah would come suddenly at midnight, as their forefathers obtained their deliverance at that very hour (Ex. xii. 29). But it is probable that midnight is named simply because that is the time when deep sleep falls upon men; and because thus the unexpectedness of Christ's coming (1 Thess. v. 2) is set forth in a lively manner.

When the cry was heard, *then all those virgins arose, and trimmed their lamps.*6 Every one at the last prepares to give an account of his works, seriously searches whether his life has been one which will have praise of God. Many put off this examination to the last moment, but beyond the day of judgment at farthest it cannot be delayed. When the day of Christ comes, a flood of light shall pour into the darkest corners of all hearts, so that self-deception will be no longer possible. Thus when the foolish virgins arose to trim their lamps, they discovered, to their dismay, that their lamps were about going out, and they had no more oil; so that they were compelled to turn to their companions. *Give us of your oil, for our lamps are gone* (or, as the margin says correctly), *going out.*7 The request and the refusal, like discourse between Abraham and Dives, are only the clothing of this truth—that we shall look in vain from men for that grace which God alone can supply. We cannot borrow that which must be *bought*—won, that is, by earnest prayer and diligent endeavor.

But the wise answered, saying, Not so; lest there be not enough for us and you. Every man must live by his own faith. There is that which one can communicate to another, and make himself the richer; but there is also that which, being Divine, is in its very nature incommunicable from man to man, and which every man must obtain for himself. The wise virgins gave the best counsel they could when they said, *Go ye rather to them that sell, and buy for yourselves:* turn to them whom God has appointed in the Church, as channels of his gifts, or, as some would explain it, to the apostles and prophets, and learn from their teaching how to revive the work of God in your souls, if yet there be time. We see in the words, *lest there be not enough for us and you,* an argument against works of supererogation. The wise virgins did not feel that they had anything over. All which they hoped to attain was, that their own lamps might burn bright enough to allow them to make part of the bridal company.

While the others were absent, seeking to repair past neglect, *the bridegroom came, and they that were ready,* they whose lamps were burning, *went in with him to the marriage,*8 *and the door was shut*—that Door, says one, which saith, "Him that cometh to me, I will in no wise cast out." Behold how it is now open, which shall then be closed for evermore. Murderers, publicans, harlots all come, and they are all received, but then—the door is shut. No one's penitence, no one's prayer, shall be any more admitted (Luke xvi. 26). The door once shut, *afterwards came the other virgins, saying, Lord, Lord, open to us;* Having sought for the oil in vain, they come looking for mercy, when now it is the time of judgment. In the title *Lord* they claim to stand in intimate relation with the bridegroom; while in the repetition of the title, we see an evidence of their earnestness in seeking admission. But *he answered and said, Verily, I say unto you, I know you not.* It is not that he disclaims outward knowledge, but he does not know them in that sense in which the Lord says, "I know My sheep, and am known of Mine." Augustine says profoundly, it is nothing else than "Ye know not Me." The issue is that the foolish virgins remain forever excluded from the marriage feast (Isa. lxv. 13). On this Bengel observes, that there are four classes of persons: those that have an *abundant* entrance into the kingdom; those that are saved, as shipwrecked mariners with difficulty reaching the shore: On the other side, there are those who go evidently the broad way to destruction, whose sins go before them; while again there are those who, though they seemed not far from the kingdom, yet miss it after all. Such was the fate of these five foolish virgins, and it is the most miserable of all. Lest that may be our fate, the Lord says to us, *Watch therefore, for ye know neither the day nor the hour* (the rest of verse has no place in the text) ; "and this being so, the only certain way of being ready upon *that* day, is that you be ready upon *every* day. Unreadiness upon that day is without remedy. That which should have been the work of a life cannot be huddled into a moment. *Watch therefore, for ye know neither the day nor the hour."*

It is quite true that there is one great coming of the Lord at the last; yet not the less does He come in all the great crises of His Church. He came at Pentecost; the prudent in Israel went in with Him to the feast, the foolish tarried without. He came at the Reformation, when the same thing took place.

A few words may be said on the relation which this parable bears to the Marriage of the King's Son, and how it happens that in that the unworthy guest actually finds admission to the marriage supper, while here the foolish virgins are not admitted to the feast. It is probable that the marriage festivities which are spoken of there, are different from these. In Gerhard's words, "Those are celebrated in this life in the Church militant, these at the last day in the Church triumphant. To those, men are called by the trumpet of the Gospel; to these, by the trumpet of the Archangel. To those, who enter, can again go out from them, or be cast out; who is once introduced to these, never goes out nor is cast out—wherefore it is said, *The door was shut."*

CHAPTER XIV.

THE TALENTS

Matt. xxv. 14-30.

WHILE the virgins were represented as *waiting* for their Lord, we have here the servants *working* for him. There by the end of the foolish virgins we were warned against declensions in the spiritual life; here against slothfulness in our outward work. It is, therefore, with good reason that the parable of the Virgins precedes this of the Talents, since the sole condition of a profitable outward work for God, is that the life of God be diligently maintained in the heart. Or we may consider the distinction between the two as this: that the virgins are the more contemplative, the servants the more active working members of the Church. This is no doubt the same discourse with that in Mark xiii. 34. St. Luke (xix. 11) has recorded for us a parable similar to this, but not identical. The time and places are different; the one in Luke having been spoken when Jesus was drawing near to Jerusalem; this, while seated on the Mount of Olives, the third day after His entry into the city. That was spoken to the multitude as well as to His disciples; this in the innermost circle of His most trusted followers. The scope of the parable in Luke is twofold. It is addressed in part to the giddy multitude, who were following Jesus with high temporal expectations, and who when disappointed might turn and join in the cry, "Crucify him." He warns them, that His triumph, if not speedy, should yet be certain and terrible over His enemies, and it contains for them a double warning, that they be not prevented from attaching themselves to Him yet closer by the things which should befall Him at Jerusalem; and that, least of all, they should suffer themselves to be numbered among His foes, since these were doomed to destruction. It has an admonition for the disciples, also, that this long period before His coming again in glory and power, was not to be for them a time of sloth, but a time in which to show all good fidelity to their absent Lord.

To no other than the Apostles was the parable of the Talents spoken. We must keep in mind the relation of masters and slaves in antiquity. Slaves then were often allowed to engage freely in business, paying a fixed yearly sum to their masters; or, as here, they had money given them, wherewith to trade on his account, or with which to enlarge their business, bringing him in a share of the profits. Here, something of the kind is assumed. *The kingdom of heaven is as a man travelling into a far country, who called his own servants, and delivered to them his goods* (it should not be "his *own* servants;" for there is no emphasis in the original). It was *a far country* into which our Lord was about to travel, and that His servants might be furnished in his absence. He was about to intrust to them many excellent gifts. The day of Pentecost was doubless the time when the goods, *i. e.* the spiritual powers and capacities, were most abundantly communicated (Eph. iv. 8-12). Yet the Saviour had communicated much to them while He was on earth (John xv. 3 and xx. 22), and from that day He has been ever delivering His goods to each successive generation of His servants. Hence, although this parable was first addressed to the Apostles alone, it has reference to all times; and as all Christians are intrusted with gifts, for which they will have to render an account, the parable is applicable to all. And these gifts are not spiritual merely, for wealth, reputation, ability, are given to men to be turned to spiritual ends; and for the use of these also will a reckoning be held with their possessors. There is a witness for this in our word *talent,* which has come to signify any mental faculties or endowments whatever.

But these gifts are in different proportions: *Unto one he gave five talents, to another two, and to another one: to every man*

according to his several ability. The natural is the ground upon
which the spiritual is superinduced. Grace does not dissolve the
ground-work of individual character. (1 Cor. xii. 4-31; Eph. iv.
16). The natural gifts are as the vessel, which may be either
large or small, but in each case is filled. The one who received
two talents might be unfitted for such a sphere of labor as he
who had received five, but he was fully supplied for that to
which he was destined, for "there are diversities of gifts, but the
same Spirit;" and as in an army all are not generals, so in the
Church all are not furnished to be leaders. But in speaking of
natural capacity, we must not forget that comparative unfaith-
fulness will narrow the vessel, even as faithfulness has a tendency to dilate it.

Having thus made all his arrangements, the lord *straightway
took his journey.* The three verses following embrace the whole
period between the first and second coming of Christ. The two
faithful servants are the representatives of all that are diligent
in their office and ministry, whatsoever that may be. In this
parable the faithful servants multiply their unequal sums in the
same proportions: *He that had received the five talents, made
them other five talents . . . ;* while in the parable recorded by
St. Luke, the servants multiply their equal sums in unequal
proportions. The truth as brought out in St. Matthew is, that
according as we have received will it be expected from us; and
that in St. Luke, that as men differ in fidelity and zeal, so will
they differ in the amount of their spiritual gains. But, *He that
had received one* talent, *went and digged in the earth, and hid
his lord's money,* — an apt image for neglect to use divinely
imparted gifts.

*After a long time the lord of those servants cometh and
reckoneth with them.* In the joyful coming forward of the faithful
servants, we see an example of boldness in the day of judgment;
they had something to show, as Paul earnestly desired that he
might have (1 Thess. ii. 19; 2 Cor. i. 14; Phil. iv. 1). In St.

Matthew the servant says, *Behold I have gained . . .* while in St. Luke it is, "Thy pound hath gained;" thus they make up the speech of St. Paul, "I— yet not I, but the grace of God that was with me." The commendation of the servants is in the same language, even as their gain was in the same proportion to their talents—five for five and two for two. *Enter thou into the joy of thy lord*—that is, become a sharer of my joy. Leighton says very beautifully here: "It is but little we can receive here, some drops of joy that enter into *us;* but there *we* shall enter into joy, as vessels put into a sea of happiness." No doubt the underlying image is that the master celebrates his return by a great festival. It is well known that under certain circumstances the master's inviting his slave to sit down with him at table, did itself constitute the act of manumission; henceforth he was free. Perhaps there may be here allusion to something of the kind. "Henceforth I call you not servants . . . " (John xv. 15; Luke xii. 37; Rev. iii. 20).

But he to whom only one talent had been given, is the one who is found faulty—a solemn warning to how many, since this excuse might occur to such: "So little is committed to my charge, that it does not signify what becomes of it." But the Lord looks for fidelity in little as well as in much. It is true he had not been guilty in the same way as the Prodigal Son wasting his substance, nor was he ten thousand talents in debt like the Unmerciful Servant; but this parable is not for those who are by their lives denying that they count Christ as their master at all: the warning is for them who *hide* their talent. There is great danger that such persons may deceive themselves; for there is a show of humility in the excuses often made by persons so inclined: "The care of my own soul is sufficient to occupy me wholly; while I am employed about the souls of others, I may perhaps be losing my own." This was repeatedly the case in the history of the early Church. Augustine, on the other hand, makes striking use of this parable, while speaking of the temptation of which he was conscious, to withdraw from active labor, and to cultivate a solitary piety: "Nothing is better, nothing sweeter," he says, "than to search the divine storehouse with none to disturb. To preach, to argue, to build up, to take care of each one, is a great load, great toil; who would not escape from it? But the Gospel deters."

The root out of which this mischief grows, is laid bare in the words, *Lord, I knew thee, that thou are a hard man.* It has its rise, as almost every thing else that is evil, in a false view of the character of God. This speech is not a mere excuse, but it is the out-speaking of the heart. The churl who accounted his lord churlish thought him even such an one as himself. But to know God's name is to trust in Him. They indeed who undertake any work for God know that they shall commit many mistakes, and perhaps sins, which they might avoid, if they declined the work altogether; but would they not by so doing testify that they thought that their Master was a hard lord, making no allowances, and never accepting the will for the deed, but watching to take advantage of the least failure on the part of His servants?

In these words, *reaping where thou hast not sown, and gathering where thou hast not strawed,* he gives evidence that he has also entirely mistaken the nature of the work to which he was called. (*Where thou hast not strawed,* or better, *scattered* with the fan on the barn-floor, there expectest thou to *gather* with the rake,—as one who will not be at the trouble to purge away the chaff, yet expects to gather in the golden grain.) He thought it something to be done *for* God, instead of being a work to be wrought *in* Him, or rather which He would work in and through His servants. Aquinas says truly, "God requireth from man nothing but the good which Himself hath sowed in us;" and Augustine, in a prayer: "Give what Thou dost command, and command what Thou wilt."

The servant goes on to say, *I was afraid;* he justifies his timidity; he feared to trade, lest he should lose all, and thus incur his master's displeasure. *Lo, there thou hast that is thine.* In reality, God's gifts cannot be so restored, for keeping the negative precepts only is not enough. But his lord answers him on his own grounds, not seeking to justify himself from the charges made against him: *Thou wicked and slothful servant; thou knewest that I reap where I sowed not, and gather where I had not strawed;* yet even then thou art not cleared; for thou oughtest to have done me justice still: *Thou oughtest therefore to have put my money to the exchangers, and then at my coming I should have received mine own with usury.* This is explained by Olshasen thus: "Those timid natures which are not suited to independent labor in the kingdom of God, are here counselled to attach themselves to other stronger characters, under whose leading they may lay out their gifts to the service of the Church."

His doom is now pronounced. First, *Take therefore the talent from him.* We have here a limitation of Rom. xi. 29. This deprivation may be considered partly as directly penal, and partly as the *natural* consequence of his sloth; for as in the natural world a limb never exercised loses its strength, so the gifts of God unexercised fall away from us: *From him that hath not shall be taken away even that which he hath.*[1] On the other hand, the gifts of God are multiplied by being laid out: *Unto every one which hath shall be given, and he shall have abundance* (Heb. vi. 7). And not only is this the case, but *that very gift* which the one loses the other receives. We see this continually; by the providence of God, one steps into the place and opportunities which another has left unused, and so has forfeited (1 Sam. xv. 28). And herein is mercy, that it is not done all at once, but little by little; and there is always a warning, "to strengthen the things which remain, that are ready to die." But this servant had never seen his danger until it was too late; and he not merely should forfeit his talent, but also, *Cast ye the unprofitable servant into outer darkness; there shall be wailing and gnashing of teeth.*

The foolish virgins erred through a vain over-confidence; this servant, through an under-confidence that was equally vain and sinful. Thus we see the two opposing rocks on which faith is in danger of making shipwreck. These virgins thought it too easy a thing to serve the Lord—this servant thought it too hard. The class to which they belong, need such warnings as this: "Strait is the gate and narrow is the way that leadeth unto life, and few there be that find it" (Matt. vii. 14; Phil. ii. 12; Matt. xvi. 24). He was representative of a class needing the following: "Ye have not received the spirit of bondage again to fear" (Rom. viii. 15; Heb. xii. 18, 22, 24).

CHAPTER XV.

THE SEED GROWING SECRETLY

Mark iv. 26-29.

THIS is the only parable which is peculiar to St. Mark. It seems to occupy the place of the Leaven, and besides what it has in common with that parable, declares further, that this word of the kingdom has that in it which will allow it to be safely left to itself. The main difficulty is this: Who is this man casting seed into the ground?—is it the Son of Man Himself, or those ministers and others who declare the Gospel of the kingdom? If we say that the Lord means Himself, how can it be said that He knows not how the seed springs and grows up? since it is only by His Spirit in the heart that it grows at all. Neither can He be compared to one who sows seed, and then goes away and is occupied with other business; for He is not merely the author and finisher of our faith, but also conducts it through all its intermediate stages. Or, on the other hand, if we say that by the sower is meant one of the inferior messengers of the truth, how shall we reconcile the words at ver. 29, *When the fruit is brought forth, immediately he putteth in the sickle, because the harvest is come?* Of whom can this be said, save of the Son of Man, the Lord of the harvest? So that, on the one hand, we meet a diffculty when we call the sower the Son of Man, by attributing to Him something less than appertains to Him; and, on the other hand, if we take the sower to be inferior ministers, we attribute to them something which can only belong rightly to Him. I cannot see any perfectly satisfactory way of escape from this perplexity. It will hardly do to say that ver. 27 belongs only to the drapery of the parable, for it is the very point and moral of the whole.

I will, however, take the parable as having reference in the first place, though not exclusively, to the Lord Himself. It begins thus: *So is the kingdom of God, as if a man should cast seed into the ground, and should sleep, and rise night and day.* By these last words is signified an absence of after-carefulness; he sleeps securely by night, and by day is about his ordinary business. Meanwhile, the *seed should spring and grow up, he knoweth not how.* These words have no difficulty, so long as we apply them to those who are teachers in the Church. They are here bidden to have faith in the seed which they sow, for it is the seed of God; when it has found place in a heart, they are not to be tormented with anxiety concerning the final issue, but to have confidence in its indwelling power; for God undertakes to maintain its life. They are also to be content that the seed should grow up without their knowing exactly how; the mystery of the life of God in any heart is unfathomable. It has a law indeed, *First the blade, then the ear . . .* but that law is hidden. It is not, of course, meant that they are not to follow up their work;[1] but then it is a different thing to impart life, and to impart the sustenance for life.

But in what sense can that which is said of leaving the seed to itself be affirmed of Christ? Olshausen suggests the following: It is true, he says, that the spiritual life of men is never at any time without the care and watchfulness of the Lord who first gave that life; yet there are two moments when He may be said especially to visit the soul—at the beginning of spiritual life, which is the seed-time, and again when He takes His people to Himself, which is their time of harvest. Between these times, the work of the Lord is going forward—not, indeed, without the daily supply of His Spirit, but He does not appear so plainly as at those two cardinal moments. We see this even more in the growth of the Universal Church. The Lord, at His first coming in the flesh, planted a Church in the world, which having done, He withdrew Himself. Often since that time has it appeared to man as if the Church were at its last gasp, yet He has not come forth. He has helped it to surmount all obstacles, but without visible interference. He has left the divine seed to grow on by night and by day, and only when the harvest of the world is ripe, when the number of the elect is accomplished, will He appear the second time unto salvation, reaping the earth, and gathering the wheat into His barns.

Our Lord's object in using the words, *The earth bringeth forth fruit of herself,* is pointedly to exclude the continuous agency of the sower.[2] The three stages of spiritual growth implied in the *blade, the ear, the full corn in the ear,* suggest a comparison with 1 John ii. 12-14. With ver. 29 we may compare Rev. xiv. 14, 15. The entire parable gives the same encouragement which St. Peter means to give when he addresses the faithful in Christ Jesus (1 Pet. i. 23-25).

CHAPTER XVI.

THE TWO DEBTORS

Luke vii. 41-43.

IT is tolerably certain that the accounts of our Lord's anointing, given in Matt. xxvi. 7, Mark xiv. 8, and John xii. 3, all refer to the same event. But whether St. Luke narrates the same circumstances, and whether the woman here, *which was a sinner,* be Mary, the sister of Lazarus, which must then follow, is a more difficult question. There are three main arguments for the identity of all the relations: first, the name of Simon as the giver of the feast; secondly, the seeming unlikelihood that twice the Lord should have been so unusually honored; and thirdly, the coincidence that in each case some one should have taken offence.

But it may be answered that the name Simon was of too frequent use among the Jews, for any stress to be laid upon the sameness of the name. Again, the anointing of the feet, though not so common as the anointing of the head, still was not without precedent; the only remarkable coincidence here being that each of these women should have wiped our Lord's feet with the hairs of her head. But if we take it as an expression of homage and love, then its recurrence is nowise wonderful. And such it is; in the hair is the glory of the women; in the human person it is highest in place and honor, while the feet are the lowest. This service, then, was but the outward expression of the inward truth, that the chiefest of man's glory was lower than the lowest that belonged to the Son of God. Yet it was an honor with some differences in the motives which called it forth. In the case of Mary, the sister of Lazarus, the impelling cause was intense gratitude: Christ had crowned His spiritual gifts to her by giving back her beloved brother; the costly ointment was a thank-offering, and as less of shame was mingled in her feelings, she anointed her Lord's head as well as His feet. But it was the earnest yearning after forgiveness that brought this woman to the feet of Jesus, and she, in her deep shame, presumed to anoint only His feet, standing the while behind Him; and in kissing them and wiping them with the hair of her head, she realized the bidding of St. Paul (Rom. vi. 19). Finally, although in each case there was an offence taken, yet in the one case, it is the giver of the feast who is offended — and he at our Lord; while in the other it is principally Judas — and he against the woman rather. To all this it may be added, that there is no probability that the Mary of the happy family in Bethany had ever been one to whom the title of *sinner,* as here meant, could be applied.[1] The passage, then, containing the parable of the Two Debtors, will be considered without any reference to the accounts in the other Gospels, of which, indeed, I have the firmest conviction that it is altogether independent.

Our Lord having been invited to the house of a Pharisee, had there *sat down to meat.* That a woman, uninvited, and of such a character, should have pressed into the chamber, and should have been permitted to offer such homage to the Saviour, may at first sight appear strange; but it can easily be explained when we remembering that in the East the meals are often almost public.[2] We must remember her present earnestness, too. In the thoughts which passed through Simon's heart, we see the true spirit of a Pharisee: of one who would have said, had the woman dared to approach *him,* "Stand by thyself, for I am holier than thou!" In the conclusion to which he came, "This man, if he were a prophet, would have known who and what manner of woman this is," we trace the current belief of the Jews, that discerning of spirits was an especial mark of the great prophet, the Messiah — a belief founded on Isa. xi. 3, 4. Thus Nathanael (John i. 48, 49; see also John iv. 29). The Pharisee thought: Either he does not know the character of this woman, in which case he lacks the discernment of a true prophet; or if he knows it, and yet accepts a service at such hands, he is lacking in that holiness, which also is a mark of a prophet of God. But the Lord satisfied him of His discernment by laying his finger on the tainted spot of *his* heart. *Simon, I have somewhat to say unto thee.* He could not refuse to listen — *Master, say on.* With this leave to speak, the parable is uttered:

There was a certain creditor which had two debtors: the one owed five hundred pence, and the other fifty. And when they had nothing to pay, he frankly forgave them both. God is the creditor, men the debtors, and sins the debts. *Tell me, therefore, which of them will love him most? Simon answered, I suppose that he to whom he forgave most.* Difficulties meet us when we come to the application of these words. Are we to conclude that there is any advantage in having multiplied transgressions? the more sin, the more love? And to understand the passage thus, would it not be to affirm a moral contradiction — to affirm that the deeper man's heart is sunk in selfishness and sensuality, the more capable he will be of the highest and purest love?

But all will be clear if we consider the debt, not as so many outward transgressions, but as so much conscience of sin. Often they who have the least of what the world calls crime (for the world knows nothing of sin), have yet the deepest sense of the exceeding sinfulness of sin, and, therefore, are the most thankful for the gift of a Redeemer. But he who has little forgiven is not necessarily he who has sinned little, but he who is lacking in any strong conviction of the great evil of sin, who has never learned to take home his sin to himself; and who, therefore, while he may have no great objection to the plan of salvation, yet thinks he could have done nearly or quite as well without Christ. He loves little, because he has little sense of deliverance wrought for him.

Simon himself was an example of one who thus loved little; and he had betrayed this lack of love in small yet insignificant matters. He had withheld from his guest the ordinary Eastern courtesies, had neither given Him water for His feet (Gen. xviii. 4), nor offered Him the kiss of peace (Gen. xxii. 4), nor anointed His head with oil, as was customary at festivals (Ps. xxiii. 5). But this woman had far exceeded them. She had washed the Saviour's feet with her tears, and wiped them with the hairs of her head; she had multiplied kisses, and those upon the feet; while she had with precious ointment anointed even his feet.

Wherefore I say unto thee, Her sins, which are many, are forgiven: for she loved much; but to whom little is forgiven, the same loveth little. There is here an embarrassment, how to reconcile these words with the parable, where the debtor is said to love much, because forgiven much, and not to be forgiven much, because he loved much; and again, to make them agree with the Scriptural doctrine, that we love God because He first loved us — that faith, and not love, is the pre-requisite for forgiveness.[3]

But the words, *for she loved much,* may best be explained by considering what the strong sorrow for sin, and earnest desire for forgiveness, mean, and from whence they arise; surely, from this, from the deep feeling in the sinner's heart, that by his sins he has separated himself from that God who is Love, while yet he cannot do without His love; from the feeling that the heart must be permitted to love Him, and be again assured of His love toward it, else it will die. Sin unforgiven is felt to be the great barrier to this; and the desire after forgiveness, if it be not a mere selfish desire for personal safety, is the desire for the removal of this barrier, that so the heart may be free to love, and to know itself beloved again; it is the flower of love desiring to bloom, but afraid of the chilling atmosphere of the anger of God,—but which will do so at once, when the genial spring of His love succeeds. In this sense that woman *loved much.* On account of this, which in fact was *faith* (ver. 50), she obtained forgiveness of her sins. This sense of emptiness, this feeling and acknowledgment that a life apart from God is not life, but death, with the conviction that in God is fulness, which He is willing to impart to all who bring the empty vessel of the heart to be filled by Him; this, call it faith, or initiatory love, is what that Pharisee, in his legality and pride, had scarcely at all, and therefore he derived little or no good from communion with Christ. But that woman had it in large measure, and bore away the best blessing, even the forgiveness of her sins. In her it was proved true that "where sin abounded, grace did much more abound."

CHAPTER XVII.

THE GOOD SAMARITAN

Luke x. 30-37.

WE need not suppose that the lawyer who "stood up," and proposed to our Lord the question out of which this parable grew, had any malicious intentions, nor even a desire to perplex and silence the Saviour. The question, "What shall I do to inherit eternal life?" was not an ensnaring one. He is said, indeed, to have put the question to Christ, "tempting him." But to tempt properly means to make trial of, and whether the tempting be good or evil, is determined by the motive from which it springs. Thus God tempts man, when he puts him to the proof, that He may show him what is in himself (James i. 12) ; He tempts man to bring out his good, and to strengthen it (Gen. xxii. 1) ; or if to bring his evil out, it is that the man may himself know it, and watch and pray against it: only Satan tempts man purely to bring out his evil. Compare Matt. xxii. 35 with Mark xii. 28-34—both records of the same conversation. In the second account, our Lord bears witness of the questioner, that he was a seeker after truth. This lawyer would fain make proof of the skill of the Galilean teacher, and thus brought forward the question of questions.

Our Lord in substance says,—The question you ask is already answered. "How readest thou?" That the lawyer should at once lay his finger on the great commandment which Christ Himself had quoted on that other occasion, showed spiritual insight; that he was superior to the common range of his countrymen. He cites Deut. vi. 5 in connection with Lev. xix. 18. Thereupon our Lord says, "Thou hast answered right; *this do, and thou shalt live,*"—let what thou knowest pass from dead knowledge into living practice, and it will be well. Still the

109

lawyer would justify himself: "True, I am to love my neighbor as myself; but who is my neighbor?"[1] This very question, like Peter's (Matt. xviii. 21), was one involving a wrong condition of mind. He who asked, "Whom shall I love?" proved that he did not understand what love meant; for he wished to have it known beforehand where he should be at liberty to stop, while the very essence of love is, that it has no limit, except in its own inability to proceed further, that it is a debt which we must be forever paying (Rom. xiii. 8).

The Saviour's reply is wonderful in its adaptation, leading him to take off his eye from the object to which love is to be shown, and turning it inward upon him who is to show the love; for this is the key to the following parable: *A certain man went down from Jerusalem to Jericho.* These words are used not merely because Jerusalem stood higher than Jericho, but because the going to Jerusalem, as the metropolis, was always spoken of as going up (Acts xviii. 22). The distance between the two cities was about a hundred and fifty stadia (eighteen miles), the road lying through a desolate and rocky region. St. Jerome mentions that a certain part of this road was called the red or the bloody way, so much blood had there been shed by robbers. Such as these *stripped him of his raiment, wounded him, and departed, leaving him half dead.*

As he lay bleeding in the road, *by chance* (or "by coincidence," as the original would imply), *there came down a certain priest that way.* Thus is shown the fine weaving in, by God's providence, of the threads of different men's lives into one common woof. He brings one man's emptiness into relation with another's fulness. Many of our calls to love are of this kind; and perhaps they are those which we are most in danger of missing, by failing to see in them the finger of God. This priest missed *his* opportunity. He may have been to Jerusalem, accomplishing his term of service, and now on his way home; but he was one who had never learned, "I will have mercy, and not

sacrifice." For *when he saw him, he passed by on the other side.*
So also did a Levite, but his conduct was even worse; for he
looked, and saw the miserable condition of the man, and yet
afforded him no assistance. Thus did these two, who made their
boast, and were the express interpreters, of the law. (Compare
Deut. xxii. 4; Ex. xxiii. 5.) Here not a brother's ox, but a
brother himself, was lying in his blood, and they hid themselves
from him (Isa. lviii. 7).

But a certain Samaritan,[2] *as he journeyed, came where he was.*
He was exposed to the same dangers as the others, and might
have made the same excuses: the sufferer was beyond the help
of man, the robbers were perhaps not far distant; if found
near him, he might be accused of being the murdered. But he
heeded not these selfish fears, for *he had compassion on him.*
It was left to the excommunicated Samaritan, whose name even
was a by-word of contempt among the Jews, to show what love
was; and this not to a fellow-countryman, but to one of a hostile
race, one that cursed his people. All the influences which had
surrounded him, probably, would have led him to repay hate
with hate. For if Jews heaped indignities on Samaritans, yet
Samaritans were not behindhand in insults to Jews. Josephus
says that they sometimes fell upon and murdered those who were
going to Jerusalem.

But the heart of this Samaritan was not hardened, although
every thing must have been at work to steel it against the
distresses of a Jew. The minuteness of the details here is exceedingly touching. He *bound up his wounds,* no doubt with portions
of his own garments, having first poured in wine to cleanse them,
and then oil to allay their smart; these two being costly, but
highly esteemed, remedies throughout the East. All this took
some time; but after he had thus revived in him the dying spark
of life, he *set him on his own beast, and brought him to an inn,*
and there again renewed his attention. Nor did he feel as if he
had done all, for *he took out two pence, and gave them to the*

*host, and said unto him, Take care of him, and whatsoever thou
spendest more, when I come again I will repay thee.*[3]

Beautiful as this parable is, taken according to the letter only,
and full of incentives to active mercy and love, yet we find much
more beauty, and much greater motives to love, when we see the
work of Christ portrayed to us here.[4] Christ, He who accounted
Himself every man's brother, fulfilled the law of love in its
largest extent, showing how we ought to love, and whom; and
inasmuch as it is faith in His love towards us, which alone causes
us to love one another fervently, He might well propose Himself
and His act in succoring the perishing humanity, as the everlasting pattern of self-denying love. The present leaders of the
theocracy had not healed the sick, nor sought that which was
driven away (Ezek. xxxiv. 4), while He had bound up the
broken-hearted (Isa. lxi. 1), and poured the balm of consolation
into wounded spirits.

The traveller, then, is personified human nature, or Adam
as the representative of the race. He has left Jerusalem, the
heavenly city, and is travelling towards Jericho, the city under
a curse (Josh. vi. 26). But he no sooner turns his desires towards
the world, than he falls under the power of him who is both a
robber and a murderer (John viii. 44), and by him is stripped
of his original righteousness, and left grievously wounded, every
sin a gash from which the life-blood of his soul is flowing. Yet
he is not altogether dead. When the angels fell, it was by a self-
determining act of their own will, with no outward temptation,
and therefore there was no possible redemption for them. But
man is *"half* dead;" he has still a conscience; evil is not his
good, however little he may be able to resist its temptations; he
still feels as if he had lost something, and has at times a longing for that which is lost. As concerns his own power to help
himself, his case is desperate, but not when taken in hand by a
Divine Physician. And who else but such an one can give back
to him what he has lost? Can the law do it? "If there had been

a law which could have given life, verily righteousness should have been by the law" (Gal. iii. 21). The priest and the Levite —the law and the sacrifices—were alike powerless to help. Gillebert says: "Abraham passed us by, for he was himself justified in the faith of one to come. Moses passed us by, for he was not the giver of grace, but of the law. Aaron the priest passed us by, and by sacrifices which he offered was unable to purge the conscience from dead works to serve the living God. Thus patriarch, prophet, and priest passed us by. Only that true Samaritan was moved with compassion, and poured oil, that is, Himself, into the heart, purifying all hearts by faith" (Rom. viii. 3).

We might say with Chrysostom, that the wine is the blood of the Passion, the oil the anointing of the Holy Spirit.[5] On the *binding* up of the wounds, we notice that the Sacraments are often spoken of in the early Church as the *ligaments* for the wounds of the soul. But Augustine says: "It is the stanching of the ever-flowing fountain of evil in the heart." When we find the Samaritan walking by the side of his own beast, upon which he had placed the wounded man, we are reminded of Him who for our sakes became poor, that we through His poverty might be rich. We may see in the inn the figure of the Church, in which the healing of souls is ever going forward. We find Christ's work spoken of in the Scriptures as a work of healing (Mal. iv. 2; Hos. xiv. 4; Ps. ciii. 3; Matt. xiii. 15).

And if, like the Samaritan, He is not always in body present with those whose cure He has begun, He yet makes a rich provision of grace for them during His absence. As the Samaritan took money and gave to the host, saying, *Take care of him,* even so the Lord Jesus said to Peter, and in him to all his fellow-apostles, having first richly furnished them for their work, "Feed my sheep . . . " To all that succeed them, also, He has committed an economy of the truth, that they may dispense the mysteries of God, for the health and salvation of His people.

And as it was said to the host, *Whatsoever thou spendest more, when I come again I will repay thee;* so the Lord has promised that no labor shall be in vain in Him (1 Peter v. 2, 4).

It is with exceeding great wisdom that the Saviour, having brought this parable to an end, reverses the question of the lawyer, and asks, *Which now of these three, thinkest thou, was neighbor unto him that fell among the thieves?* He had asked, "Who is the neighbor to whom I am bound to show love?" The Lord's lesson was this: it is not the object which is to determine the love, but that love has its own measure in itself; it is like the sun, which does not ask on what it shall shine, or what it shall warm, but shines and warms by the very law of its own being, so that there is nothing hidden from its light and heat. The lawyer had said, "What marks a man as my neighbor?" The Lord holds up before him a despised Samaritan, who, instead of asking that question, freely exercised love towards one who certainly had none of the signs such as the lawyer conceived might mark out a neighbor in his sense of the word. The parable is not a reply to the question, but to the spirit from which the question proceeded. It was an appeal to a better principle in the querist's heart, from the narrow and unloving theories in which he had been trained.

And now in answer to our Lord's question, "Which was neighbor?" he says, *He who showed mercy on him. Go,* the Lord says, *and do thou likewise.* He would make the lawyer aware of the great gulf between his knowing and his doing — how little his actual exercise of love kept pace with his knowledge of the debt of love due from him to his fellow-men, a point on which his question, "Who is my neighbor?" shows a secret misgiving.

CHAPTER XVIII.

THE FRIEND AT MIDNIGHT

Luke xi. 5-8.

THE disciples had just asked, "Lord, teach us to pray," and our Saviour graciously gives them that perfect form which is the treasure of the Church. But He also instructs them in what spirit they are to pray, even in that of persevering faith: There is this difference between this parable and that of the Unjust Judge, that here the selfishness of man is set against the liberality of God, while there it is his unrighteousness tacitly contrasted with the righteousness of God. The conclusion is, that if selfish man can yet be won by importunity to give, how much more certainly shall the bountiful Lord bestow, "who both is sleepless, and when *we* sleep rouses us to pray" (Augustine). Here, also, it is prayer for the needs of others in which we are bidden to be instant; while there it is rather for our own needs. Yet we must not, in either case, urge the illustration too far; for though God may present Himself *to us* in aspects similar to these, yet His is only a *seeming* neglect, while theirs is *real*. We see an illustration of this seeming unwillingness in the conversation with the Syro-Phœnician woman (Matt. xv. 21), and also in the history of Jacob wrestling with the angel (Gen. xxxii. 24-32).

Which of you shall have a friend, and shall go unto him at midnight, and say unto him, Friend, lend me three loaves: for a friend of mine, in his journey, is come to me, and I have nothing to set before him. I do not see any deeper meaning in these words than lies on the surface; yet they have given rise to many beautiful allegorical interpretations. It has been said that the guest is the spirit of man, weary of wandering, suddenly desiring heavenly food. But the host, that is, man in his sensual nature, has nothing to give, and is here taught to appeal to God, that he may receive spiritual nourishment for the soul. Vitringa explains it thus: The guest is the heathen world; the host, the servants and disciples of Jesus, who are taught that they can only nourish it with the bread of life, as they themselves receive it from God,—which they must therefore seek with all perseverance. In like manner, of the three loaves it has been said that the host craving this number, craves the knowledge of the Trinity, or perhaps, the three gifts of the Spirit—faith, hope, and charity.

The words which he from within replies, *Trouble me not, the door is now shut,* mean more than that it is merely closed; it is barred and fastened, and this is an unseasonable hour. *I say unto you, though he will not rise and give him because he is his friend, yet because of his importunity, he will rise and give him as many as he needeth.* The word translated *importunity,* means rather *shamelessness.* But this shamelessness is mitigated by the thought that it is not for himself, but that he may not be wanting in the rites of hospitality to another. Abraham's conversation with God (Gen. xviii. 23-33) illustrates it. Through this pertinacity he finally obtains, not merely three, but *as many as he needeth;* like the Syro-Phœnician woman: "Be it unto thee even as thou wilt." Augustine observes, that he who would not at first send even one of his house, now rises himself, and supplies the wants of his friend.

The parable concludes with a commendation of the same duty of persevering prayer: *And I say unto you, ask, and it shall be given you; seek, and ye shall find; knock, and it shall be opened unto you.* This is not mere repetition, for to seek is more than to ask, and to knock is more than to seek; and thus an exhortation is given to *increasing* urgency in prayer, even till the suppliant carries away the blessing which God is only waiting for the proper time, to give. "The kingdom of heaven suffereth violence, and the violent take it by force."

CHAPTER XIX.

THE RICH FOOL

Luke xii. 16-21.

IN the midst of one of our Lord's most interesting discourses, an interruption occurs. One of His hearers had so slight an interest in the spiritual truths which He was communicating, was so concerned about a wrong which he believed himself to have sustained, that he broke in upon the Lord's teaching with that request which gave occasion for this parable, "Master, speak to my brother, that he divide the inheritance with me." From his appeal to Jesus, made in the presence of the whole multitude, it is probable that his brother was really treating him unjustly. But it was the extreme inopportuneness of the season for urging his claim, that showed him as one in whom the worldly prevailed to the danger of exclusion of the spiritual,[1] and that drew a warning from our Lord. He declined in this, as in every other case, to interfere in the affairs of civil life. His adversaries had sought to thrust upon Him the exercise of a jurisdiction which He carefully avoided. See John viii. 1-11, and Matt. xvii. 24-27. But each time He avoided the snare, keeping Himself within the limits of the moral and spiritual world, as that from which alone effectual improvements in the outer life of man could proceed. He would work from the inward to the outward.

Our Lord, having uttered a warning against covetousness, a sin always united with the *trusting* in uncertain riches, shows by a parable the folly of such trust. For, besides other reasons, security is necessary to blessedness; but that earthly life, which is the necessary condition of drawing enjoyment out of worldly abundance, may come to an end at any moment. *The ground of a certain rich man brought forth plentifully.* "The prosperity of fools shall destroy them;" a truth to which this man sets his seal, for his prosperity draws out his selfish propensities into stronger action. It might, indeed, seem as if we should be in the greatest danger of setting our heart upon riches, when we saw them escaping from our grasp. But all experience testifies that earthly losses are the remedy for covetousness, while increase in worldly goods serves not as water to quench, but as fuel to increase, the fire (Eccl. v. 10).

He thought within himself, saying, What shall I do? Here we are admitted to the inner chamber of a worldling's heart, rejoicing over his abundance, and making "provision for the flesh, to fulfil the lusts thereof." *I have no room where to bestow my fruits.* "Thou *hast* barns—the bosoms of the needy, the houses of the widows, the mouths of orphans and of infants" (Ambrose).[2] This would have been his wisdom thus "to bestow" his wealth; but he does not thus provide for himself "bags which wax not old, a treasure in the heavens which faileth not;" but, *I will pull down my barns, and build greater, and there will I bestow all my fruits and my goods.* "Observe," says Theophylact, *"my* goods and *my* fruits." His riches were fairly got, and this makes the example the better to suit the present occasion. The world would see nothing to condemn in his plans for future enjoyment: *I will say to my soul, Soul, thou hast much goods laid up for many years: take thine ease, eat, drink, and be merry.* He determines now to rest from his labors. His plans of happiness rise no higher than to the satisfying of the flesh, and there is a melancholy irony in making him address this speech to his *soul*—to that soul which was capable of knowing and loving and glorifying God.

He expects thus to nourish his soul *for many years;* he thinks as Job did once, to multiply his days as the sand. "But God said unto him, *Thou fool, this night thy soul shall be required of thee."*[3] *Thou fool,* opposed to his own opinion of his prudence,— *this night,* to the many years which he had promised himself,—and that *soul* which he had purposed to make fat, shall be *required* of him. We are not to suppose any direct manifestation in the idea of God's speaking to this man, but what is more awful, that while those secure plans were going on in his thoughts, this sentence was being determined in the counsels of God. Not *as yet* was there any direct communication between God and the man's soul, but even at the very moment when God was pronouncing the decree that the thread of his life should in a few minutes be cut in twain, he was confidently promising to himself a long period of uninterrupted security.

There is a force in *shall be required of thee.* Theophylact: "For from the righteous his soul is not *required,* but he commits it to the Father of spirits, pleased and rejoicing." The mere worldling is torn from the world, which is his only sphere of delight, as the fabled mandrake was torn from the earth, shrieking and with bleeding roots. *Then whose shall those things be, which thou hast provided?* Solomon, long before, had noted this uncertainty as constituting part of the vanity of wealth (Eccl. ii. 18, 19; comp. Ps. xxxix. 6).

So is he that layeth up treasures for himself, and is not rich toward God, or, does not enrich himself towards God,—for the two clauses of the verse are parallel. Self and God are here contemplated as the two poles between which the soul is placed, for one of which it must determine, and then make that one the end of all its efforts. The man laying up treasure for himself, while that is made the end and object of his being, is impoverishing himself inwardly; for there is a continual draining off to worldly objects of those affections which were given him that they might be satisfied alone in God; where his treasure is, there his heart is also. He that has no love of God, and no share in the unsearchable riches of Christ, is in fact "wretched, and miserable, and poor, and blind, and naked," however he may say, "I am rich and increased with goods, and have need of nothing." On the other hand, he who is rich toward God and in God, possesses all things, though a beggar in this world, 'and will, when he dies, not quit, but go to, his riches.

Our Lord, having thus warned His hearers against covetousness, and knowing how often it springs from a distrust in God's providential care, teaches them (ver. 22-30) the love and care of a heavenly Father. In the 24th verse, we have, perhaps, a distinct reminiscence of this parable.

CHAPTER XX.

THE BARREN FIG-TREE

Luke xiii. 6-9.

THE insurrectionary character for which the Galileans were noted, may have been the excuse for the outrage mentioned in ver. 1, which must have been perpetrated at Jerusalem, for there alone sacrifices were offered. Those who narrated it to our Lord probably meant to suggest that if men could be safe anywhere, it would be at God's altar, but that there must have been some great hidden guilt, which rendered the very sacrifices of these men to be sin, so that they themselves became piacular expiations, their blood mingling with, and forming part of, those which they offered. But our Lord at once laid bare the evil in their hearts, rebuking their cruel judgments. "Suppose ye, that these Galileans were sinners above all the Galileans, because they suffered such things?" He does not deny that they were sinners, but He does deny that their calamity marked them out as sinners *above all others*[1] of their fellow-countrymen; and then He leads His hearers (comp. Luke xiii. 23; John xxi. 22) to take their eyes off from others, and fix them upon themselves. "Except ye repent, ye shall all likewise perish." We are here taught that in the calamities which befall others, we have loud calls to repentance, for we are to recognize that whatever befalls another, might justly have befallen ourselves. Moreover, when we have learned to see the root of sin in ourselves, we shall learn to acknowledge that whatever deadly fruit it bears in another, it might have borne the same or even worse, in like circumstances, in ourselves. One who feels thus will not deny, as neither does our Lord deny, the intimate connection between sin and suffering, but it is the sin of the race which is linked with the suffering of the race; not, as necessity at least, the sin of the individual with his particular suffering.

Our blessed Lord, to set the truth yet more plainly before His bearers, brings forward another instance of a swift destruction falling upon many at once:—"Those eighteen on whom the tower of Siloam fell and slew them, think ye that they were sinners above all men that dwelt in Jerusalem?" In these accidents, in this disharmony of nature, all were to recognize a call to repentance, for all such events are parts of the curse consequent on the sin of man. There is a force in the original word, which our English "likewise" fails to give. The threat is that they shall literally *in like wise* perish. Multitudes of the inhabitants of Jerusalem were crushed beneath the ruins of their temple and city; and during the last siege and assault, there were numbers also, who were pierced through with Roman darts in the courts of the temple, in the very act of preparing their sacrifices, so that literally their blood was mingled with their sacrifices.

Olshausen observes:—"The discourse of Jesus, severe and full of rebuke, is closed by a parable, in which the merciful Son of man appears as the Intercessor for men before the righteousness of the Heavenly Father; as He who obtains for them space for repentance. This idea of deferring the judgment of men, runs all through the Holy Scriptures (Gen. vi. 3; Gen. xviii. 24) ; the destruction of Jerusalem was not until forty years after the ascension of our Lord (see also 2 Pet. iii. 9)." This parable, then, is at once concerning the long-suffering and severity of God.

A certain man had a fig-tree planted in his vineyard. Though by the fig-tree the Jews are directly meant, yet as Israel according to the flesh was the representative of all and of each who in after times should be admitted to the principles of a nearer knowledge of God, so is a warning herein contained for the Gentile Church, and for every individual soul. The possessor of the fig-tree *came and sought fruit thereon, and found none* (Isa.

v. 2, 7; Jer. ii. 21). The simple image of men compared to trees, and their work to fruits, runs through the whole of Scripture (Ps. i. 3; John xv. 2, 4, 5; Rom. vii. 4). There are three kinds of works spoken of in the New Testament, which may all be illustrated from this image: first, *good* works, when the tree, being made good, bears good fruit; then *dead* works—fruit, as it were fastened on from without, alms given that they may be gloried in, prayers made that they may be seen . . . ; and lastly, *wicked* works, when the corrupt tree bears fruit manifestly of its own kind.

Of the *three years* in which the master of the vineyard complains that he finds no fruit, many explanations have been given. Theophylact:—"Christ came three times—by Moses, by the Prophets, and in His own person." Augustine understands by them the times of the natural law—the written law—and now, of grace. Olshausen thinks they may refer to the three years of our Lord's ministry upon earth; but Grotius had already observed, that if so, the one year more must also be chronological, whereas forty years were allowed before the final destruction of the Jews. *Cut it down* (Isa. v. 5, 6; Matt. vii. 19); *why cumbereth it the ground?* (We miss here the *also* of the original, after the word "why." It is really the key-word of the sentence.) St. Basil beautifully says: "This is peculiar to the clemency of God toward men, that He does not bring in punishments silently or secretly; but by His threatenings first proclaims them to be at hand, thus inviting sinners to repentance." Before the hewing down begins, the axe is laid at the root of the tree (Matt. iii. 10). The cumbering of the ground implies more than that it occupied a place which might be more profitably filled; the barren tree injured the land around. Thus, the Jewish Church not merely did not bring forth fruits of righteousness, but through them the name of God was blasphemed among the Gentiles (Rom. ii. 24; Matt. xxiii. 13, 15). So is this true of the individual sinner;

that he is not only unprofitable to God, but, by his evil example, he is a stumbling-block to others.

The dresser of the vineyard, who pleads, *Lord, let it alone this year also,* is manifestly the Son of God Himself (Job xxxiii. 23; Zech. i. 12; Heb. vii. 25) ; yet not as though the Father and Son had different minds concerning sinners, as though the counsels of the Father were wrath, and of the Son mercy. But at the same time we must not fall into the opposite error, letting go the reality of God's wrath against sin, and the reality of the sacrifice of Christ on that side which looks towards God; the death of Christ was really a propitiation of God, not merely an assurance of God's love towards sinners. We see the way of escape from both of these errors in those words: "The Lamb slain from the foundation of the world" (Rev. xiii. 8) ; "foreordained before the foundation of the world" (1 Pet. i. 20) ; we must not conceive of man as ever not contemplated by God in Christ (Rom. xvi. 25, 26). In this view we may consider the high-priestly intercession of Christ as having found place and been effectual even before He passed into the heavens—before He had carried His own blood into the truly Holy of Holies.

The vine-dresser pleads not that the barren tree may stand forever, though it continue barren; for he consents to its doom, if it remain unfruitful; but he asks for it one year of grace; *If it bear fruit, well; and if not, then after that thou shalt cut it down.* During this year, *he will dig about it, and dung it;* that is, he will hollow out the earth from around the stem, and fill up the hollow with manure; as one may often see done now to orange-trees in the south of Italy. By this is signified the multiplication of the means of grace, which God gives before they are withdrawn forever. Thus before the flood, Noah appeared a "preacher of righteousness,"—before the great catastrophes of the Jews, some of their most eminent prophets appeared,—and before the final destruction of Jerusalem, they enjoyed the ministry of Christ and His Apostles. To this last, allusion is here no doubt immediately made, to that larger, richer supply of grace, consequent on the death, resurrection, and ascension of our Lord. Doubtless this is true of men's lives as well.[2]

Such a time of visitation to the Jewish nation was our Lord's ministry (Luke xix. 42). There was the digging about the tree which had so long been barren. But it abode in its barrenness, and, as was threatened, was cut down. Yet our Lord's words, *If it bear fruit, well,* show that there was another alternative. The door of repentance is left open to all; they are warned that it is only themselves who make their doom inevitable.

CHAPTER XXI.

THE GREAT SUPPER

Luke xiv. 15-24.

IT has already been proved that this parable and the one recorded at Matt. xxii. 2 are entirely different. On the present occasion our Lord had been invited to eat bread at the house of one of the chief Pharisees (ver. 1). This was probably an expensive entertainment; from the various circumstances related in verses 7 and 12, we may conclude that many were present, and, it is likely, guests of consideration. This supposition adds much force to the admonishment (ver. 12). Our Lord's words in ver. 14, "Thou shalt be recompensed at the resurrection of the just," called forth from one present the admiring exclamation, "Blessed is he that shall eat bread in the kingdom of God!" The Jews believed that the resurrection of the just, the open setting up of the kingdom of God, would be ushered in by a great festival, of which all the members of that kingdom should be partakers. This, therefore, was an earthly way of saying, "Blessed and holy is he that hath part in the first resurrection." He spoke these words, it is likely, with an easy assurance that he should be one of the privileged number. He, as a Jew, a member of the elect nation, had been invited to that great feast of God; he did not pause to consider whether he had truly accepted the call, and certainly he had not considered whether in the refusal to enter into the higher spiritual life, to which Christ was inviting him, there was not involved his own final rejection from the heavenly festival. To him, and to others like him, the parable was spoken.

A certain man made a great supper. Men's relish for heavenly things is so little that they are presented to them under such inviting images as this, that, if possible, they may be stirred up to a more earnest longing after them. *And bade many,* these were, as the latter part of the parable indicates, the priests, elders, scribes, and Pharisees. These, as claiming to be following after righteousness, seemed to be pointed out as the first who should embrace the invitation of Christ. The maker of the feast *sent his servant at supper-time, to say to them that were bidden, Come, for all things are now ready.* This was the usual custom, and their contempt of the honor done them, and neglect of their given word,—for we must suppose that they had already accepted the invitation,—are testified by the excuses which they make for not appearing at the festival. There was, without doubt, a time when more than any other it might be said, *all things are now ready,* a fulness of time, when the kingdom of heaven was set up, and men were invited to enter into it, first the Jew, and afterwards the Gentile. By the servant sent to bid the guests is not meant our Saviour; neither does he represent the prophets, for it is not till *all things are now ready,* that he is sent forth. He rather represents those who accompanied the Saviour, preachers, evangelists, apostles, and all who, reminding the Jews of the ancient prophecies concerning the kingdom of God, and their share therein, bade them now enter on the enjoyment of these good things.

And they all with one consent (or, out of one mind or spirit) *began to make excuse.* Perhaps he who said *I have bought a piece of ground, and I must needs go and see it,* represents those who are elate of heart through acquired possessions.[1] It adds much to the earnestness of the warning of the parable that none of the guests are kept away by occupations in themselves sinful, and yet all become sinful, because the first place is given to them. While with him it is "the lust of the eye and the pride of life" (Dan. iv. 30), which keep him from Christ, in the second it is rather the care and anxiety of business which fill the soul; *I have bought five yoke of oxen, and I go to prove them.* This trial of the oxen was probably to take place before the purchase was finally concluded. He is getting what the other has already got. In the last we see that it is the pleasure of the world that keeps him from Christ: "See you not that I have a feast of my own? why trouble me with yours? *I have married a wife, and therefore I cannot come."* This one accounts that he has a reason perfectly good, and therefore does not trouble himself with the words, *I pray thee, have me excused,* but bluntly refuses. As in Matt. xxii. so here, there is an ascending scale. The first would be very glad to come, if it were possible; the second alleges no such necessity of absence, but is simply going upon sufficient reason in another direction; yet he too prays to be excused. The third has plans of his own, and says outright, *I cannot come.* In what remarkable connection do these excuses stand with the words of our Lord, which follow so soon after (verse 26), and how apt a commentary does St. Paul supply (1 Cor. vii. 29-31). They had nothing which it was not lawful to have, but the undue love of earthly possessions ultimately excluded them from the feast.—The servant returns and declares to his lord, how *all* have excused themselves from coming; even so it was said, "Have any of the rulers or of the Pharisees believed on him?" (John vii. 48). *Then the master of the house, being angry, said to his servant, Go out quickly into the streets and lanes of the city, and bring in hither the poor, and the mained, and the halt, and the blind.* We have here a distinct reminiscence of ver. 13. Thus is it with the great Giver of the heavenly feast. He calls the spiritually sick and needy, while those who are rich in their own merits exclude themselves and are excluded by Him. The publicans and sinners, the despised and outcast of the nation, should enter into the kingdom of God before those who thanked God they were not as other men.

Hitherto the parable has been historic, now it passes on to the prophetic, for it declares how God had prepared a feast, at which more shall sit down than a remnant of the Jewish people—that He has founded a Church in which there would be room for Gentile as well as Jew. Not that this is explicitly declared, but is wrapt up in the parable. The servant, returning from his second mission, had said, *Lord, it is done as thou hast commanded, and yet there is room,* whereupon, since grace will endure a vacuum as little as nature, he receives a new commission, *Go out into the highways and hedges, and compel them to come in, that my house may be filled.* If those in the lanes of the *city* are not most miserable and sinful of the Jews, then those *without* the city—in the country around—will be the yet more abject Gentiles, the *pagans* in all senses of the word. Concerning these, the word is, *Compel them to come in.* Of course this means a moral compulsion. It is not implied that there would be any indifference toward the invitation, but that these houseless wanderers would think themselves so unworthy of it as not to believe it, and could scarcely be induced without much persuasion to enter the rich man's dwelling, and share in his entertainment.

And since faith cannot be *compelled,* this word must be applied to that strong, earnest exhortation which the ambassadors of Christ will address to men when they are themselves deeply convinced of the importance of their message and of the great results depending. If they *compel,* it will be as the angels compelled Lot (Gen. xix. 16) ; or they will, in another way, compel men to come in, for they will speak the words of Him who not merely entreats, but commands, all men everywhere to repent and believe the Gospel. As Luther explains it, men are compelled to come in when the law is preached, terrifying their consciences, and driving them to Christ as their only refuge. The parable closes with the indignant exclamation of the householder, *For I say unto you that none of those men that were bidden, shall taste of my supper;* this is the penalty with which he threatens them—no after earnestness in claiming admission shall profit them (Prov. i. 28; Matt. xxv. 11, 12). This exclusion is nothing less than exclusion from the kingdom of God, and from all the blessings of the communion of Christ, and that implies "everlasting destruction from the presence of the Lord, and the glory of His power."

This whole parable suggests a parallel with 1 Cor. i. 26-29.

CHAPTER XXII.

THE LOST SHEEP

Matt. xviii. 12-14; Luke xv. 3-7.

WHEN St. Luke says, "Then draw near to the Lord all the publicans and sinners for to hear him,"[1] we must understand him as giving the prevailing feature in the whole of Christ's ministry, or at least in one epoch of it. The publicans were hateful to their countrymen, being accounted as traitors who for the sake of filthy lucre had sided with the Romans, the oppressors of the theocracy, and now collected tribute for a heathen treasury. No alms might be received from their money-chest; their evidence was not taken in courts of justice, and they were put on the same level with heathens (this fact gives an emphasis to Luke xix. 9). By the word "sinners" is meant all those who, till awakened by the Lord to repentance, had been notorious transgressors. Being come to seek and to save that which was lost, He received them graciously, and lived in familiar intercourse with them. At this the Scribes and Pharisees took offence. They could have understood a John the Baptist flying to the wilderness to escape contamination, but Christ was the physician who rather came boldly to seek out the infected, in order to heal them. The Pharisees had neither love to hope for the recovery of such, nor medicines to effect it.

Their murmurings were the occasion of the three parables which follow. Christ holds up to them God and the angels of God rejoicing at the conversion of a sinner, and silently contrasts this with their envious repinings. More than this, He warns them that if they indulge in this proud self-righteousness, there will be *more* joy in heaven over one of these penitents whom they despised, than over ninety-nine of such as themselves. He does not deny the good that might be in them; but if now

133

they refused the higher righteousness of faith, the new life of the Gospel, then such as would receive this life from Him, though having in times past departed infinitely wider from God than they had done, would now be brought infinitely nearer to Him.

The first two parables set forth mainly the *seeking* love of God; while the third describes to us rather the rise and growth of repentance responsive to that love. The three would have seemed incomplete if separated, for the two first speak nothing of a changed heart toward God, nor indeed would the images used have allowed of this; while the last speaks only of this change, and nothing of that which must have caused it, namely, the antecedent working of the Spirit of God in the heart. But there are also many other inner harmonies between them, interesting to trace. The possessor of a hundred sheep, in some sort a rich man, was not likely to feel the loss of a single one so deeply as the woman who, out of ten small pieces of money, should lose one; and her feelings would come infinitely short of the parental affection of a father who, having but two sons, should behold one of them going astray. Thus we find ourselves moving in ever narrower, and so ever intenser circles of hope, and fear, and love — drawing thus nearer to the innermost centre and heart of the truth.

We see also, in each case, shadowed forth a greater guilt, and therefore a greater grace. In the first parable, the sinner is set forth as a silly wandering sheep. Though this is but one side of the truth, yet it is a most real one, that sin is oftentimes an ignorance; the sinner knows not what he does. Multitudes of wanderers go astray, before they have even learned that they *have* a shepherd. But there are others, set forth under the lost money, who, having known themselves to be God's, and to be stamped with the image of the Great King, do yet throw themselves away, and renounce their high birth. But there is a sin yet greater — the sin of the prodigal — to have known something of the love of God, not as our King, but as our Father, and yet to have slighted that love, and forsaken His house — this is the crowning guilt; and yet the grace of God is sufficient to reclaim even such a wanderer.

The first parable had a peculiar fitness to the spiritual rulers of the Jewish people. They were warned, rebuked, and charged continually under this very title of shepherds (Ezek. xxxiv.; Zech. xi. 16) ; yet now they were finding fault with Christ for doing that very thing which they ought to have done. There is in sin a *centrifugal* tendency, and of necessity the wanderings of the sheep would be farther and farther away. Therefore, without the shepherd's going forth to seek it, it must be lost forever. We are not to understand by the *wilderness* in which the ninety-nine sheep were left, any thing more than wide-extended grassy plains, called desert because without habitations of men. Thus we read in John (vi. 10) that there was much grass in a place which another Evangelist calls a desert. So that the residue of the flock are left in their ordinary pasturage, while the shepherd seeks the lost sheep.

Christ's Incarnation was a girding of Himself to go after His lost sheep. In His own words, He "came to seek and to save that which was lost." And He sought His own *till* He *found it*. He followed us into the deep of our misery. And having found his sheep, the shepherd does not punish it, nor even harshly *drive* it back into the fold, but he lays it upon his own shoulders and carefully carries it home. In this last we see an image of the supporting grace of Christ, which ceases not till His rescued are made partakers of final salvation. And as the man reaching home summons friends and neighbors to share his joy, so Christ declares there shall be joy in heaven on the occasion of one sinner repenting. Though not distinctly declared, He lets it sufficiently appear, that it is even Himself who, returning to the heavenly places, shall cause jubilee there. For we must notice, that this joy of which He speaks is future; He has not yet risen

and ascended, leading captivity captive, and bringing with Him
His redeemed. Nor let us miss the intimation of the dignity of
His person given in *I say unto you* — I who know, I who tell
you of things which I have seen (John iii. 11), I say to you that
this joy shall be in heaven.

Were this all the declaration, there would be nothing to
perplex us; but there is *more* joy over the penitents *than over
ninety and nine just persons which need no repentance.* We can
easily understand how, *among men,* there should be more joy for
a small portion which has been endangered, than for the continued secure possession of a much larger portion. More joy is
felt upon the recovery of a sick friend, even though as yet it be
not entire, than when he walked sound and strong. Yet this
disproportionate joy arises clearly from the unexpectedness of
the result, from the temporary uncertainty of it. But God who
knows the end from the beginning needs not to have a joy
heightened by a fear going before.

Still further, the words, *which need no repentance,* are difficult, since we read, *"All* we like sheep have gone astray." We
may indeed get rid of both difficulties by seeing here an instance
of our Lord's severe yet loving irony, and finding in the ninety
and nine the self-righteous. But the whole construction of the
parable is against such a supposition; the ninety and nine sheep
have *not* wandered. The one view which affords a solution is this
— that we understand these *righteous* as really such, but that
their righteousness is merely legal. The law had done a part of
its work for them, keeping them from gross positive transgressions of its enactments, but it had not brought them, as God intended it should, to a conviction of sin; it had not prepared them
to embrace the salvation offered by Christ. He now declares that
there was more real joy over one of these publicans and sinners,
who were entering into the inner sanctuary of faith, than over
ninety and nine of themselves, who lingered at the legal vestibule,
refusing to enter. Gregory the Great observes: "A general in

battle prefers that soldier who, turning back from flight, charges the enemy bravely, to him who never fled, and never showed any valor."

CHAPTER XXIII.

THE LOST PIECE OF MONEY

Luke xv. 8-10.

IT WOULD be against all analogy of preceding parables to presume that this, and the one that has gone just before, although so much alike, say merely the same thing. If the shepherd in the last parable was Christ, the woman in this may, perhaps, be the Church, or the Divine Wisdom which so often in Proverbs is described as seeking the salvation of men, and is here as elsewhere set forth as a person (Luke xi. 49). Rather these two explanations flow into one, when we keep in mind how the Church is the organ in and through which the Holy Spirit seeks for the lost. Keeping the fact prominently in view that it is only as the Church is dwelt in by the Holy Spirit, that it can appear as the woman seeking her lost, and that it is only as the Spirit says "Come," that the Bride can say it, we shall have in the three parables the three Persons of the Holy Trinity, although not in their order.

In the lost piece of money, expositors have traced a resemblance to the human soul ("God created man in His own image," Gen. i. 27), which still retains traces of the mint from which it proceeded, though the image has been nearly effaced by sin; farther, as the piece of money is lost for all useful purposes to its owner, so man through sin has become unprofitable to God. But as the woman, having lost her piece of money, will *light a candle, and sweep the house, and seek diligently till she find it,* even so the Lord, through the ministrations of the Church, gives diligence to recover the lost sinner. The lighting of the candle may be explained by such passages as Matt. v. 14; Phil. ii. 15. The candle is the word of God, which the Church holds forth; and it is by this light that sinners are found — that they find themselves, and the Church finds them. Having this candle, she proceeds to sweep the house, deranging every thing for a time. The charge evermore is that the world is turned upside down. But amidst all the outcry, she that bears the candle of the Lord ceases not from her labor, until she has recovered her own again.

We must not omit to remark a difference between this parable and the preceeding, which is more than accidental. In that the shepherd sought his lost sheep in *the wilderness;* but it is in *the house* that the piece of money is lost and looked for. There is, then, a progress from that to this. The visible Church now first appears. There are other variations also, to be explained on the same supposition that we have there the more immediate ministry of Christ, and here the secondary ministry of His Church. The shepherd says, "I have found *my* sheep;" the woman, "I have found *the* coin;" for it was not hers in the sense in which the sheep was his. He says, "which *was* lost;" she says, "which *I* lost," confessing a fault of her own, the original cause of the loss; for a sheep strays of itself, but a piece of money could only be lost by a certain negligence on the part of possessor.

The woman having found her own, *called her friends and her neighbors together,* that they may share her joy. We have in the next verse our Lord's warrant for applying this to the angels, whose place is not "in heaven," as in the last parable: for this is the rejoicing together of the redeemed creation *upon earth* at the repentance of a sinner. The angels that walk up and down the earth, that are present in the congregations of the faithful— there shall be joy before them when the Church of the redeemed, quickened by the Holy Spirit, summons them to join with it in thanksgiving for the recovery of a lost soul; for, as St. Bernard says, the tears of penitence are the wine of angels.

CHAPTER XXIV.

THE PRODIGAL SON

Luke xv. 11-32

THIS might be called the pearl and crown of all the parables of Scripture; one containing within itself such a circle of doctrine as abundantly to justify the title sometimes given it of *Evangelium in Evangelio,* The Gospel within the Gospel. In respect to its primary application, there have always been two different views; some considering the sons as the Jew and the Gentile, the younger representing by his conduct the apostasy and return of the Gentile world, the elder, the narrow-hearted, self-extolling Jews, grudging that the "sinners of the Gentiles" should be admitted to the same blessing with themselves; others looking upon the younger son as representing *all* who have widely departed from God, and who having in consequence experienced misery, have by His grace been brought back to Him, while in the elder brother they see either a narrow form of real righteousness, or one righteous in his own sight, not in the Lord's. The latter view is the more correct one, though not rigorously excluding the former. The parables in this chapter are spoken by Jesus to justify His conduct in receiving "publicans[1] and sinners," who were Jews, and not to unfold that far deeper mystery, the calling of the Gentiles, of which he gave only a few hints to His chosen disciples, and which was for a long time a stumbling-block even to them.

The younger of these two sons said to his father, Give me the portion of goods that falleth to me. We *need not* conceive of his asking this as a right, though it may have been so, but only as a favor. The portion, according to the Jewish law, would be the half of what the elder brother would receive (Deut. xxi. 17). In a spiritual sense, this request is an expression of man's desire to be independent of God (Gen. iii. 5), of his desire to take the ordering of his life into his own hands, believing that he can be a fountain of blessedness to himself. All subsequent sins are included in this one. We express the feeling directly opposed to this in the words, "Give us this day our daily bread," in which we acknowledge that we desire to wait continually upon God for the supply of our bodily and spiritual needs.

The father *divided unto them his living.* It would have little profited to retain *him* at home, who had already in heart become strange to that home. Such is the dealing of God; He has constituted man a being with a will; and when His service no longer appears a perfect freedom, and man promises himself liberty elsewhere, he is allowed to make the trial, and to discover that in departing from Him he falls under the horrible bondage of his own lusts and of the world, and under the tyranny of the devil. And now, the younger son is

"Lord of himself—that heritage of woe."

Yet although he had gained his portion, he did not immediately leave his home. St. Bernard sees a force in this, and observes how the apostasy of the heart will often precede the apostasy of the life. The divergence of the sinner's will and the will of God does not immediately appear. Soon, however, it must, for *not many days after, the younger son gathered all together, and took his journey into a far country.* By this gathering together of all, and departing, seems intimated the collecting on man's part of all his energies, with the deliberate determination of getting all that he can out of the world. The *far country* is a world where God is not, or, as Augustine has it, "The 'far country' is forgetfulness of God." There he *wasted* or scattered *his substance with riotous living,* so quickly has the *gathering* issued in a *scattering.*

The supplies lasted for a while, and he may have congratulated himself upon his liberty. Even so the sinner does not discover at once his misery and poverty; for the world has its attractions, and the flesh its pleasures. But the time arrives when he comes to the end of all that the creature can give him; *when he had spent all, there arose a mighty famine in that land and he began to be in want.*[2] He begins to discover his misery, and that it is an evil thing and a bitter to have forsaken the Lord his God (Jer. ii. 19; xvii. 5, 6). In the spiritual world, there *need be,* though often there will be, no outward calamities to bring on this sense of famine. It sits unbidden at rich men's tables, and enters into kings' palaces. *There,* the immortal soul may be ready to *perish with hunger.*

If we see here the great apostasy of the heathen world, as well as the departure of a single soul, this wasting of goods will be exactly that in Rom. i. 19-23, as the remainder of the chapter will exactly answer to the residue of the prodigal's sad experience. The great famine of the heathen world was at its height when the Son of God came in the flesh. All childlike faith in the old religions had departed. The Greek philosophy had failed.

That the prodigal *began to be in want,* was, no doubt, a summons to him to return home, but as yet his confidence in his own resources was not altogether exhausted. *He went and joined himself to a citizen of that country,* hoping to repair his broken fortunes by his help. And here we see a fall within a fall — a more entire yielding of himself by the sinner to the service of the world. Still, this prodigal with all his misery was not yet a *citizen* in that far country. There is hope for the sinner so long as he feels himself a miserable alien in the land of sin. By his *joining himself* to the citizen, our Lord gives us a hint of that dark mystery in the downward progress of souls, by which he who begins by using the world as his servant to minister to his pleasures, ends by becoming its slave.

But sinful man finds no love, no pity from his fellow-sinner. This new master dismisses him from his sight, and sends him to the vilest employment, *to feed swine.* We know that it was even accursed in the eyes of a Jew; so that the prodigal's cup of misery was full. And now, *he would fain have filled his belly with the husks that the swine did eat; and no man gave unto him.* (These *husks* are not the pods of some other fruit, but themselves the fruit of the carob tree. They are very common in the Levant. The shell or pod alone is eaten.) This is generally taken as meaning that he could not obtain even these husks; but seeing they must have been in his power, we may suppose that *he did* eat them, no man giving him any thing more satisfactory.[3] The expression *filled his belly,* is chosen of design—all he could do was to dull his gnawing pain, for the food of beasts could not appease the cravings of man. So, also, none but God can satisfy the longings of an immortal soul.

The whole description is wonderful; we see the evident relation in which his punishment stands to his sin. "He who would not be ruled by God, is compelled to serve the devil—he who would not feed on the bread of angels, petitions for the husks of swine." In his feeding of swine, what a picture we have of man serving divers lusts and pleasures, the bestial merely predominant; and in his fruitless attempt to fill his belly with the husks, what a picture again of man seeking to satisfy the fierce hunger of the soul by the unlimited gratification of his appetites. All the monstrous luxuries and frantic wickednesses which we read of in the later Roman history, stand like the last despairing effort of man to fill his belly with husks. The experiment carried out on this largest scale only proved that the food of beasts could not be made the nourishment of men.

It is true that this picture, if applied to more than a few, is an exaggeration of the misery and wickedness of those who have turned their backs upon God; but yet it is also true, that all this misery and sin are rendered possible by, and are the legitimate results of, a first departure from God; and nothing hinders them from following, but the restraining grace of God. In the present case, sin is suffered to bear *all* its bitter fruit; we see one who has debased himself even unto hell. Were it not for this, it would not be a parable for all sinners, since it would fail to show that there is no extent of departure from God, which renders a return to Him impossible.

As we have followed the sinner, step by step, in his downward career, so will we now trace his return, for though he has forsaken his God, he has not been forsaken by Him. He makes his sin bitter to him, that he may leave it. In this way God pursues His fugitives, calling them back in that only language which they will now understand. Here we have one, upon whom this "stern discipline of divine mercy" (Augustine) is not wasted. Presently, *he came to himself*. How deeply significant are these words, *he came to himself* — so that to come to one's self, and to come to God, are the same thing. It is not, then, the man living in union with God, who is raised above the true condition of humanity, but the man not so living, who has fallen below that condition. God, being the true ground of our being, when and because we have found Him, we find ourselves also.

When he thus *came to himself, he said, How many hired servants of my father's have bread enough and to spare, and I perish with hunger.* This, too, is a touch of the deepest nature; for the sinner beholds everywhere but in himself peace and harmony, he sees nature calm and at rest, fulfilling in law and order the purposes for which it was ordained. He sees also many of his fellow-men, who find their satisfaction in the discharge of their daily duties; who, though doing their work more in the spirit of servants than of sons, are yet not without their reward; although they may not have the highest joy of God's salvation, they have bread enough and to spare, while he is perishing with hunger. Even at this point, how many come to a different determination from this prodigal. They betake them to some other citizen, who deludes them with false promises; or they dress their husks so that they look like human food; or they wallow in the same sty with the beasts they feed. But it is otherwise with him. *I will arise.* We may picture him as having sat long on the ground, revolving the extreme misery of his condition (Job ii. 8, 13). But now he gathers up anew his prostrate energies; "Why sit I here among the swine? *I will arise and go to my father."* These words were cited by the Pelagians of old, in proof that man could turn to God in his own strength: just as the (self-styled) Unitarians of modern times find in the circumstances of the prodigal's return a proof that the sinner's repentance alone is sufficient to reconcile him with his God—that he needs no Mediator. But these conclusions are guarded against by the clearest declarations, the first by such as John vi. 44; the second by such passages as Heb. x. 19-22; nor are we to expect that every passage in Scripture is to contain the whole circle of Christian doctrine.

Returning to that father, he *will say unto him, Father.* What is it that gives the sinner confidence, that returning to God he shall not be repelled? The adoption of sonship, which he received in Christ Jesus at his baptism, and his faith that the gifts and calling of God are without repentance or recall. He may claim anew his admission to the household, on the ground that he was once made a member thereof. *I have sinned against heaven and before thee;* he shows his repentance to have been the work of the Spirit, in that he acknowledges his sin in its root, as a transgression of the divine law, as being wrought against God. Thus David exclaimed, "Against thee, thee only have I sinned," while yet his offences had been against the second table. For we may injure ourselves by our evil, we may wrong our neighbors, but we can *sin* only against God; and the recognition of our evil as first and chiefly against Him, is of the essence of all true repentance. When we come to give these words their higher application, the two acknowledgments merge into one, "I have sinned against Thee, my Father in heaven." Throughout all Scripture this willingness to confess is ever noted as a sign of true repentance begun, even as the sinner's refusal to humble himself by this confession is the sure sign of continued hardness (2 Sam. xii. 13; Job ix. 20; Prov. xxviii. 13; Jer. ii. 35; 1 John i. 9, 10). Tertullian:—"In as far as thou hast not spared thyself, so far, believe me, will God spare thee." With this deep feeling of unworthiness, he will confess, *I am no more worthy to be called thy son.* A confession such as this belongs to the essence of all true repentance. But are the words which follow, *Make me as one of thy hired servants,* those of returning spiritual health? We shall find that at a later period (ver. 21) he drops them, and shall refer to them then.

There is no tarrying now: *He arose and came to his father; but when he was yet a great way off, his father saw him, and had compassion, and ran, and fell on his neck* (Gen. xlv. 14) *and kissed him.*[4] The evidences of the father's love are described with touching minuteness; he does not wait until his son has come all the way, but hastens forward to meet him, and at once welcomes him with the kiss, in the East the pledge of reconciliation and peace (Gen. xxxiii. 4; 2 Sam xiv. 33). Compare James iv. 8. The Lord sees His returning wanderers, while they are *yet a great way off;* He listens to the first faint sighing of their hearts after Him, for it was He that first awoke those sighings there (Ps. x. 17). And though they may be *a great way off,* though they may have far too slight a view of the evil of sin, or of the holiness of God, yet He meets them, notwithstanding, with the evidences of His reconciled love. Nor does He cause them to serve a dreary apprenticeship of servile fear, but at once embraces them in the arms of His love, giving them perhaps stronger consolations than they will have, oftentimes, after they become settled in the Christian course. And this He does because they need at this moment to be assured; notwithstanding their moral loathsomeness and misery they are accepted in Christ Jesus, a truth which it is so hard for the sinner to believe.

But although the son hears not his sin mentioned, he yet makes his confession; and this was fitting, for though God may forgive, man may not therefore forget. We must take notice that it is after, and not before, the kiss of reconciliation that the confession takes place; for, the more the sinner knows and tastes of the love of God, the more he grieves ever to have sinned against that love. And thus will repentance be a life-long thing, for every new insight into that forgiving love is a new reason for mourning that we have ever sinned against it. The true relation between repentance and a sense of forgiveness is opended to us in such passages as Ezekiel xxxvi. 31, where the Lord says, *"Then"* (and for the meaning of *then,* see ver. 24-30) "shall ye remember your own evil ways . . ." Compare Ezek. xvi. 60-63. The son does not indeed say, *Make me as one of thy hired servants,* for this shrinking back from the free grace which would restore to him all, had been the one troubled element of his repentance; and in his dropping of these words, in his willingness to be blest by his father to the uttermost, there is evidence that the grace which he has already received, has not been in vain.

And now the father showed that he meant to give him a place and a name in his house once more; for he *said to his servants, Bring forth the best robe and put it on him, and put a ring on his hand and shoes on his feet,* these being among the highest tokens of favor and honor (Gen. xli. 42). Probably by the giving of the robe is especially signified that act of God, which on the one side is a release from condemnation, and on the other an imputation of the righteousness of Christ (Zech. iii. 4). They who bring forth the robe are generally interpreted as the ministers of reconciliation. We have the gift of the Spirit indicated in the ring which is here given. In the East, the ring was used often as a seal (Est. iii. 10, 12), which naturally brings to our minds such passages as Ephes. i. 13, 14; 2 Cor. i. 22, in which a sealing by God's Spirit is spoken of.[5] The shoes also are given him, to which answers a promise (Zech. x. 12; Ephes. vi. 15). In the words, *Bring hither the fatted calf, and kill it,* I do not see, as some have done, any special allusion to the Eucharist, but more generally to the festal rejoicing in heaven at the sinner's return, and also in the Church and in the sinner's own heart.

As in the preceding parables (verses 6 and 9), so here; the householder summons his servants to share his joy. For this is the very nature of true joy—that it desires to impart itself, it runs over; and if this be true of the joy on earth, how much more of the yet holier joy of heaven! The father solemnly reinstates the wanderer, before them all, in the honors of a son. *This my son was dead, and is alive again* (Eph. ii. 1), *he was lost, and is found,* (1 Pet. ii. 25); *and they began to be merry.*

Here this parable, like the two preceding, might have ended. But our Lord, by saying *two sons,* had promised something more. It is to derive new beauty from the contrast brought out between the large heart of God and the grudging heart of man. The elder brother, while the house is ringing with festal rejoicing, returns from *the field,* where, no doubt, he had been as usual laboriously occupied. As he *drew nigh to the house, he heard music and dancing.* The singers and dancers were hired, as was the custom, on such occasions. Surprised, *he called one of the servants, and asked what these things meant.* Note how delicately his ungenial character is already indicated. He does not go in, taking it for granted that when his father makes a feast, there is good cause for merriment. He prefers to learn from a servant *what these things meant, demanding* an explanation. And then the tidings that his father had received his brother *safe and sound,*6 with the thought of his father's joy, move him rather to displeasure; *he was angry,* and in place of rushing to that brother's arms, *would not go in.*

Nor even when his father came out, and entreated him, would he lay aside his displeasure, but loudly complained, *Lo these many years do I serve thee, neither transgressed I at any time thy commandment, and yet thou never gavest me a kid, that I might make merry with my friends;* but *this thy son,*—he does not say my brother,—*which hath devoured thy living,* invidiously, for in a sense it was *his own,*—*with harlots,* very probably, yet only but a presumption on his part,—*as soon as he was come,* he says not, *was returned,* but speaks of him as a stranger—upon the first moment of his arrival, *thou hast killed for him,* not a kid, but the choicest calf in the stall. But there shall not be, if the father can help it, a cloud upon any brow, and instead of answering with severity, he expostulates, and would have him see his unreasonableness. The father's answer to the son is a warning, too, that he is falling into the very sin of his brother, when he said, *Give me the portion of goods that falleth to me,* He is feeling as though he did not truly possess what he had *with* his father. *Son, thou art ever with me, and all that I have is thine;* and then he would make him see his unloving spirit; *It was meet that we should make merry and be glad; for this thy brother* (not merely *my son,* but *thy brother*) *was dead, and is alive again; was lost and is found.*

Our view of the success of the father's expostulations, of which we are told, will be mainly determined by the interpretation which we give to this concluding portion of the parable. Those who see in the two brothers the relations of the Jew and Gentile to each other and to God, have here fewer difficulties, than the other class of interpreters. But as in the interpretation I have sought to establish, this is denied to be the *primary* object of the parable, we must look elsewhere for solution of the difficulties, which are indeed the same which beset us in the parable of the Laborers in the Vineyard. They resolve themselves into this single one: Is *their* righteousness, whom the elder brother represents, real or not? If real, how can it be reconciled with his contumacy to his father, and his unloving spirit towards his brother? and how does it agree with the aim of this part of the parable, which is directed against the Pharisees, whose righteousness, for the most part, was hypocritical? But, on the other side, if not real, how is this to be reconciled with the story, according to which the elder brother *had* remained ever in his father's house, or with his uncontradicted assertion of his own continued obedience? Each determination of the question is embarrassed with difficulties.

But there seems this possible middle course—that we see in those whom he represents, a low, but not altogether false form of legal righteousness. Such, had many of the Pharisees,—following, though in much blindness of heart, after righteousness (Rom. x. 1, 2), a righteousness indeed of a low sort, in the strivings after which they did not attain to any such knowledge of the plague of their own hearts as should render them mild and merciful to others, or thoroughly humble before God. Such may have been some of the murmurers present—in whom the good was not to be utterly denied, but who had need to be invited to renounce their servile for a filial spirit. And in this sense we must then understand the father's invitation to the elder son to come in. Hitherto, he had been laboring *in the field,* but now is invited to a festival. Those whose work for God had been the task-work of the law, are now invited to enter into the joy of the Lord, the freedom of the Spirit. Thus we have the Gospel preached to the legalist as well as to the gross sinner, love speaking in both cases.

It is plainly seen by the elder son's reply, *thou never gavest me a kid,* that he is ignorant of the nature of that kingdom to which he is uninvited. He is looking to get something *from* God, instead of possessing all things *in* God. Instead of feeling it his true reward, that he had ever been with his father, he rather would plead this as establishing his claim to some other reward. In the reply, *Son, thou art ever with me, and all that I have is thine,* we must place the emphasis not on *thou,* but on *with me.*[7] What need to talk of other friends? Thou art ever with a better than all, with myself. Why shouldest thou have expected a kid, when *all that I have is thine?* These last words wonderfully declare to us the true nature of the rewards of the kingdom. In the free kingdom of love one has not less because another has more. To each of his children the Lord says, *All that I have is thine:* if then any is straitened, it is not in God, but in his own heart.

The issue of these expostulations could not yet be told, even as it was still uncertain whether the Scribes and Pharisees might not be won to repentance. The Lord was intimating that as yet the kingdom of God was not closed against them—that they, as well as publicans and harlots, were invited to leave their poor, formal service (Gal. iv. 3, 9), and to enter into the glorious liberties of the kingdom of Christ. It is true that the refusal to go in, and on these grounds, was fearfully fulfilled, when the Jew in apostolic times refused to take part in the festival of reconciliation, with which the Gentile world's coming into the kingdom was being celebrated (Acts xiii. 45; xiv. 19; xvii. 5, 13; xviii. 12). If his brother had first been obliged to serve a painful apprenticeship to the law, it might have been different (Acts. xv. 1). But as it was, it was more than could be borne. At the same time, we Gentiles must not forget that at the end of the present dispensation all will be reversed, and that we shall be in danger of playing the part of the elder brother, and shall do so if we grudge at the largeness of the grace bestowed upon the Jew, who is now feeding upon husks, far away from his Father's house.

CHAPTER XXV.

THE UNJUST STEWARD

Luke xvi. 1-9.

THIS parable, of which the difficulties are exceedingly great, has been the subject of manifold, and those the most opposite, interpretations. I cannot doubt, however, that we have here a parable of Christian prudence, Christ exhorting us to use the world and the world's goods in a manner against itself and for God. As I proceed, I shall note the meanings given to the parable by the best interpreters, and also, what seem the weak points in those explanations which I reject.

The Lord, having finished the parable of the Prodigal Son, did not break off the conversation, but, probably after a short pause, resumed, addressing His words, not to the Pharisees, but to those who heard Him gladly,—to *His disciples.* By *His disciples,* we must not understant exclusively the twelve, nor yet the multitude which hung loosely upon Him, but rather the whole of those who having left the world's service had passed over the ranks of His people. The Pharisees, it is true, were *also hearers* of His words (ver. 14), but the very mention of them as such shows that they were not the persons to whom the parable was primarily addressed. The Lord most probably intended, however, that some of His shafts should glance off upon them.

There was a certain rich man, which had a steward. Such was Eliezer in the house of Abraham (Gen. xxiv. 2-12, and see Gen. xxxix. 4). There is not the slightest ground for supposing that the steward was falsely *accused.* This meaning does not lie in the word. Indeed, his own words (ver. 3) seem an acknowledgment of his guilt; and his after conduct will allow no conclusion, but that the accusation had its foundation in truth. The

charge against him was, that he had administered his master's
goods without due fidelity, laying them out for himself, and not
for his lord. His lord *called him, and said unto him, How is it
that I hear this of thee?—of thee,* the expostulation of indignant
surprise. *Give an account of thy stewardship, for thou mayest be
be no longer steward.*

They who, like Anselm, see in this parable the rise, growth,
and fruits of repentance, lay much stress on these words, *How
is it that I hear this of thee?* It is, they think, the voice of God
speaking to the sinner; and the threat, *thou mayest be no longer
steward,* is in like manner a warning that he will soon be removed from his earthly stewardship, and have to render an
account. He feels that when he is once removed, there will be
no help for him, and therefore he seeks, while he has time, to do
good with that which is committed to him.[1] He is, they say, still
called the "unjust" steward, not because he remains such, but for
the encouragement of penitents, like Rahab the *harlot,* etc. But
there is nothing in the man which shows repentance, but only
an utterance of fear lest poverty and distress come upon him;
and the explanation of his being still called "unjust," is quite
unsatisfactory.

But now he counsels with himself, and first he feels his helplessness; yet this does not last long. *I am resolved what to do;
that when I am put out of the stewardship they may receive me
into their houses,* as one from whom they have received kind-
nesses. Hereupon follows the collusion between him and his
lord's debtors. The two, who are spoken of here, owed, the one
a hundred measures of oil, the other a hundred measures of
wheat. We may suppose that the rich man had sold, through
his steward, a portion of his farm products to these debtors, on
credit. They were probably merchants, or other factors, who had
given their notes of hand, in which they acknowledged the
amount received, and their indebtedness to that amount. These,
which remained in the steward's keeping, he now returns to

them,—"Take *back* thy bill,"—bidding them to alter them, or make new ones, in which they should confess to having received smaller amounts of oil and wheat, and consequently to owe so much less.

In this lowering of the bills, Vitringa finds the key of the parable, and gives the following interpretation, noteworthy for its exceeding ingeniousness. The rich man is God, the steward the Pharisees, or rather all the ecclesiastical leaders of the people, who were stewards of the mysteries of the kingdom of God. But they were accused by the prophets (Ezek. xxxiv. 2, Mal. ii. 8), and also by Christ, that they used their power, not for the glory of God, but for themselves. They feel the justice of the accusation, and they now therefore seek to make themselves friends of the debtors of their Lord, of sinful men,—acting still as if they had authority. They seek to make friends by lowering the standard of righteousness and obedience, allowing men to say, "It is a gift" (Matt. xv. 5), suffering them lightly to put away their wives (Luke xvi. 18), and by various devices slack the law of God (Matt. xxiii. 16),—thus obtaining favor with men, and enabling themselves to retain their honors. This interpretation gives a distinct meaning to the lowering of the bills,— *Write fifty, Write fourscore,*—which very few others do. The moral will then be that which is commonly drawn from the parable: Be prudent as these children of this world, but while they use heavenly things for earthly objects, do you use earthly things for heavenly objects.

Connected with this view is another, according to which the unjust steward is set forth for the *Pharisees* to imitate. They were the stewards in a dispensation soon to close; and an exhortation is found here, that in the little while before the kingdom of Christ should be set up, they should cultivate that spirit which alone would give them entrance into the kingdom not to be moved, the spirit which they so much lacked, of love and meekness toward all men. But how shall this interpretation be

reconciled with the words, "He said also *unto his disciples,"*
with which the Evangelist introduces the parable?

But to return;—this child of the present world filled up the
short time remaining to him with new acts of unrighteousness.
It is not said that he attempted to conceal his fraudulent arrangement, or that he called his lord's debtors together *secretly.*
Probably, in his desperation, the thing was done openly, and
the arrangement was such as, from some cause or other, being
once completed, must be permitted to stand. Were it meant to
have been a secret transaction, the steward would scarcely have obtained even the limited praise which he does obtain as a skilful
adapter of his means to his ends. Least of all, would he have
obtained such praise, if it had depended merely on the for-
bearance of his master, in the case of discovery being made,
whether the arrangement should be allowed to stand.

But whether clandestine or not, the arrangement was certainly
a fraudulent one, and any attempt to mitigate the dishonesty
is hopeless. It may be said, indeed, that this dishonesty is not
of the essence of the parable, but an inconvenience arising from
the inadequacy of earthly relationships to set forth divine; that
while in worldly things it never can be that a servant dealing
wholly with reference to his own interests would at the same
time forward in the best manner his lord's, in heavenly things
our true interests absolutely coincide with those of our heavenly
Lord; so that when we administer the things committed to us
for Him, then we lay them out also for ourselves, and when
for ourselves, for our eternal gain, then also for Him.

*And the lord commended the unjust steward, because he had
done wisely.* It is the lord of *the steward,* who is here meant,
and not *our* Lord, who does not begin to speak directly in His
own person till ver. 9. *Wisely* is not the happiest word that
could have been chosen, since wisdom is never in Scripture
disconnected from moral goodness. *Prudently* is clearly the right
word, and is found in Wiclif's translation. Few will deny that

the phrase has something perplexing in it, not from its being incapable of a fair explanation, but from the liability of the passage to abuse, though it is not really as unguarded as at first sight it appears, for ver. 11 should never be disconnected from the parable. The explanation is clearly this: the man's deed has two sides; one, the side of its dishonesty, upon which it is most blameworthy—the other, the side of its prudence, which, if it be not particularly praiseworthy, yet is sufficiently analogous to a Christian virtue to make it the ground of an exhortation and rebuke to the followers of Christ. There are martyrs of the Devil, who put to shame the saints of God, and running as they do with more alacrity to death, than these to life (Bernard), may be proposed to them for their imitation.[2] Even so our Lord here disentangles the steward's dishonesty from his prudence; the one, of course, can only have His earnest rebuke,—the other may serve to provoke His people to a like prudence, which yet should be at once a holy prudence, and employed about things of far higher and more lasting importance.

The next verse fully confirms this view: *For the children of this world are in their generation wiser than the children of light;* that is, *more prudent.* The *children of this world* evidently means those who look not beyond this earth, being born of the spirit of the world and not of God. The phrase occurs but once else in Scripture (Luke xx. 34) ; though the term "children of light" may be found John xii. 36; 1 Thess. v. 5; Eph. v. 8. The declaration itself has been differently understood, according as the words wanting to complete the sentence have been differently supplied. Some complete it thus—*The children of this world are wiser in their generation,* namely, in worldly things, *than the children of light* are in those same worldly things; that is, earthly men are more prudent than spiritual men in earthly things; even as owls see better than eagles in the dark. But it is hard to see how a general statement of this kind bears on the parable, which most are agreed urges upon the Christian a *heavenly* prudence.

Others, then, are nearer the truth who complete the sentence thus—*The children of this world are wiser in their generation* (in worldly matters) *than the children of light* in theirs, that is, in heavenly matters; the children of light being thus rebuked that they are not at half the pains to win heaven, which the men of this world are to win earth. This is the meaning given, though too vaguely,[3] by many, for it is only perfectly seized when we see in the words, *in their generation,* or as they ought to be translated, "unto" or "towards their generation," an allusion to the debtors in the parable. They, the ready accomplices in the steward's fraud, showed themselves to be of the same generation as he was,—they were all children of the ungodly world; and the Lord's declaration is, that the men of this world make their intercourse with one another more profitable,—obtain more from it,—than do the children of light *their* intercourse with one another. For what opportunities are missed by Christians to whom a share of the earthly mammon[4] is intrusted, of laying up treasure in heaven,—of making friends for the time to come by showing love to the poor saints,—or generally of doing offices of kindness to the household of faith—to the men of the same generation as themselves!

In the following verse the Lord exhorts His disciples not to miss these opportunities,—*And I say unto you, Make to yourselves friends of the mammon of unrighteousness, that when ye fail, they may reeive you into everlasting habitations.* Some explain this *mammon of unrighteousness* as wealth unjustly gained by fraud and violence, but if so, the first recommendation would be to restore it to its rightful owners (Luke xix. 8). Others say it is not exactly wealth unjustly acquired, but that wealth which from the very nature of the world's business has somewhat of defilement clinging to it.[5] But a comparison with ver. 11, where the equivalent phrase *unrighteous mammon* is set against "*true* riches,"—heavenly, enduring goods,—makes it far more probable that the words mean the uncertain mammon, which is one man's to-day, and another's to-morrow.[6] And *mammon of unrighteousness* it may be called in a deeper sense, since it is certain that in all wealth a principle of evil is implied. In the moment of the Church's first love, "all that believed were together, and had all things common." So that though the possessor of the wealth may have fairly acquired it, yet is it not less the *unrighteous* mammon, witnessing in its very existence to the absence of that highest love which would have rendered it impossible that a *mine* and *thine* should ever have existed.

The words *that when ye fail,*[7] are, of course, equivalent to *that when ye die.* Many, however, have been unwilling to refer the words that follow, *they may receive you,* to the friends which were to be made by the help of the unrighteous mammon, as seeming to attribute too much to men and to their intercession. It has been thought by some, that *they* are the angels, and by others that God and Christ are to receive; by others, again, that the phrase is impersonal, simply meaning "you may be received." But if we look at this verse as standing in close connection with the parable, of which indeed it gives the moral, we shall see how this phrase comes to be used. The debtors, being made friends, were to receive the deposed steward into temporary habitations; and by using these words in His practical application of the parable, our Lord throws back light upon it, and at once explains to His hearers its most important part.[8] And while it is idle to assert that there will reside power of their own with the glorified saints to admit any into the kingdom of heaven, it is also idle to affirm that the words, *they may receive you,* in the second clause of the sentence, can refer to any other than the friends mentioned in the first. The true parallel to, and at once the explanation and the guard of, this passage, is Matt. xxv. 34-40.

In the verses 10-13, which stand in vital connection with the parable, it is very observable that not prudence, but faithfulness, is especially commended, so as to put far away any possible abuse of it; just as when our Saviour said, "Be wise as serpents," He immediately guarded the precept, lest it should degenerate into cunning, by adding, "and harmless as doves." Earthly things are slightingly called *that which is least,* as compared with those spiritual gifts which are *much;* they are called *that which is another man's,* by comparison with the heavenly goods, which when possessed are our own, and become a part of our very selves. In the dispensing, however, of these worldly things, He declares that a man may prove his fidelity, and will inevitably show what is in him, and whether he be fit to be intrusted with that which has a true and enduring value, namely, with a ministration in the kingdom of God. And in ver. 13, He futher states what the fidelity is, which is required in this stewardship,— it is a choosing of God instead of mammon for our lord. For in this world, we are claimed by two masters: one is God, man's rightful lord; the other is this unrighteous mammon, which was given to be our servant, to be used by us for God—but which has, in this sinful world, erected itself into a lord, and now demands obedience from us, which if we yield, we can no longer be the faithful servants of God. God, for instance, will command a scattering, when mammon will urge to a further gathering; God will require spending upon others, when mammon, or the world, will urge to a spending upon our own lusts (Jas. iv. 4) ; one must be despised, if the other is held to—it is impossible to be faithful to both: *Ye cannot serve God and Mammon.* Such appears to me to be the connection between ver. 13 and the preceding verses, and between the whole of these verses and the parable of which they are intended to give the moral.

CHAPTER XXVI.

THE RICH MAN AND LAZARUS

Luke xvi. 19-31.

HOWEVER loosely strung together verses 15-18 may at first sight appear, there is a thread of connection running through them, and afterwards joining them with the parable,—there is one leading thought throughout, namely, that in all are contained rebuke and threatening for the Pharisees. They had heard our Lord's exhortation to a liberal bounty, and they testified their scorn, whereupon He turned to them, and rebuked their hypocrisy; while they were covetous, they sought a reputation for righteousness among men. It is then announced to them (ver. 16) that that dispensation, of which they were the stewards, was passing away, and a larger dispensation, in which they should no more have the "key of knowledge" to admit or to exclude, is begun,—and "*every man* presseth into it." Not that the law itself was to be abolished, for that would be eternal as the God who gave it (ver. 17) ; and how great was their guilt, who, while pretending to guard its honor, tampered with some of its most sacred requirements, as in those concerning marriage (ver. 18) ; and thereupon the parable follows.

But, that being evidently addressed to the Pharisees, a difficulty appears. They were indeed *covetous* (ver. 14), but prodigal excess in living, like that of the rich man, is nowhere imputed to them. On the contrary, we learn from contemporary historical sources that they were remarkably abstemious. Their sins were in the main spiritual, and what other sins they had were such as were compatible with a high reputation for spirituality. Mosheim supposes the parable, therefore, to have been directed against the Sadducees; but there is no proof that any were present; nor is there any *break* between ver. 18 and 19.

The following seems to be the explanation: While it is true that covetousness, and not prodigality, was the sin of the Pharisees, yet both of these, hoarding and squandering, are so equally the consequences of unbelief in God, and in God's word, that when the Lord would rebuke their sin, He might take His example from a sin opposite in appearance to theirs. For it ought never to be forgotten, that it is not the primary purpose of the parable to teach the fearful consequences which will follow the abuse of wealth and contempt of the poor, but the fearful consequences of unbelief, of having the heart set on this world, and refusing to believe in that invisible world, here known only to faith, until by a miserable and too late experience the existence of such an unseen world has been discovered. The sin of Dives in its roots is unbelief: the squandering on self, and contempt of the poor, are only the forms which it takes. His unbelief also shows itself in supposing that his brethren, while refusing to give heed to the sure word of God, would heed a ghost. This is of the very essence of unbelief, that it gives that credence to portents which it refuses to the truth of God. Caligula, who mocked at the existence of the gods, would hide himself under a bed when it thundered; and superstition and incredulity are twin brothers. It is most important to keep in mind that this, the rebuke of unbelief, is the central thought and aim of the parable.[1]

But it is worthy of notice, that besides the literal and obvious, there has also been an allegorical interpretation of it. It has been suggested by Augustine, Theophylact, and some modern commentators, that the past and future relations of the Jew and Gentile are here set forth. Dives is the Jew, or the Jewish people, favored, self-righteous, and contemptuous of the Gentile. To the Pharisees, as the representatives of the nation, it is announced that an end is approaching, nay, has come upon them already—the former state of things is to be utterly abolished. The believing Gentiles—Lazarus—are to be brought by the messengers of the new covenant into the consolations of the Gospel; but the Jews—Dives—are to forfeit all the privileges which they have abused, and will find themselves with God's wrath abiding upon them to the uttermost.

If the present had beeen expressly named a parable, it would tend to confirm this or some similar interpretation; for according to that commonly received, it is no parable, the rich man means a rich man, and the poor man, a poor—the purple and fine linen mean just those things, and so on. Thus, in fact, the question whether this is a parable or simply a history (real or fictitious, it matters not), depends on the manner in which it is interpreted. Those, who support the allegorical interpretation, insist that it loses none of its practical value thereby, only the lower selfishness of the flesh will be used as a symbol to set forth the more spiritual selfishness; in addition to the warning to the world, there will be another deeper warning to the Church that it exalt not itself in the multitude of its own privileges, but that it have a deep and feeling sense of the spiritual wants of all who know not God, and seek earnestly to remove them. I will say more of this interpretation presently: it is not incompatible with the commonly received interpretation, to which we now return.

There was a certain rich man, which was clothed in purple and fine linen, and fared sumptuously every day,—habitually clothed, for this the word implies. The extreme costliness of the purple dye of antiquity is well known;[2] it was accounted, too, the royal color, and the purple garment was then, as now in the East, a royal gift (Esth. viii. 15; Dan. v. 7). With it, idols were often clothed (Jer. x. 9). There was pride, then, as well as luxury in its use. And the byssus, rightly translated *fine linen,* was hardly in less price or esteem. Yet, while the rich man plainly sought out for himself all that was costliest, it cannot be observed too often that he is not accused of any breach of the law, like those mentioned in Jas. v. 1-6. In Augustine's words,—"Jesus said not, a calumniator,—he said not, an oppressor of the poor,—he said not, a spoiler of orphans: nothing of these. But—*There was a certain rich man.* And what was his crime? A lazar lying at his gate, and lying unrelieved." He is not even accused of being a glutton. There is nothing to make us think of him as other than a reputable man,—one who desired to remove from himself all things painful to the flesh, to surround himself with all things pleasurable.—His name Christ has not told us, but the poor man's only.[3] "Jesus," says Cajetan, "of a purpose named the beggar, but the rich man he designated merely as *a certain man,* so to testify that the spiritual order of things is contrary to the worldly. In the world, the names of the rich are known, but the names of the poor are either not known, or if known are counted as unworthy to be particularly noted."

At the gate of this rich man, the beggar Lazarus[4] was flung —brought there, it may be, by those who counted they had done enough in casting him under the eye of one who might so easily help him. As the rich man's splendor was painted in a few strokes, so in a few as expressive is the utter misery of Lazarus set forth. Like Job, he was "full of sores,"—hungry, and no man gave to him, for it seems most probable, that he desired, but in vain, *to be fed with the crumbs which fell from the rich man's table.* He found sympathy only from the dumb animals; *the dogs came and licked his sores.* This circumstance seems mentioned to set forth the cruelty of the rich man in its strongest light;— that while he remained unmoved, even the pity of the brutes was stirred. We have in fact in the two descriptions stroke for stroke. Dives is covered with purple and fine linen; Lazarus is covered only with sores. The one fares sumptuously; the other desires to be fed with crumbs. The one (as we may imagine) has numerous attendants to humor every caprice; the other, only dogs to tend his sores.

The faith and patience of Lazarus must be assumed, since his poverty of itself would never have brought his to Abraham's bosom. In all homiletic use of this parable, this never should be left out of sight. Thus Augustine tells the poor that poverty of spirit must go along with external poverty; and he often bids them note, how the very Abraham into whose bosom Lazarus was carried, was one who on earth had been rich in flocks, and in herds, and in all possessions. "What doth it profit thee," he says, "if thou lackest opportunity and burnest with desire?"

But this worldly glory and worldly misery are alike to have an end; *It came to pass that the beggar died;* and how mighty the change! he whom none but the dogs had cared for, is now carried by angels[5] *into Abraham's bosom.* This last phrase has been sometimes explained as though he was brought into the *chiefest* place of honor and felicity. But it is rather to find its explanation from John i. 18, as a figurative phrase to express the deep quietness of an innermost communion. It is the state of painless expectation intervening between the death of Christians, and their perfect bliss at the Saviour's coming in His kingdom. It is the "Paradise" of Luke xxiii. 43, the place of the souls under the altar, Rev. vi. 9; as some distinguish it, it is blessedness, but not glory. To this haven of rest, Lazarus was safely borne.

But *the rich man also died, and was buried,* subsequently, as it would appear. Lazarus was more early exempted from the misery of his earthly lot; Dives was allowed a longer time for repentance. It is possible that the putting of Lazarus under his eye had been his final trial; his neglect of him, the last drop that made the cup of God's long-suffering to run over. He *also died and was buried.* There is a sublime irony, a stain upon all earthly glory, in this mention of his burial, connected as it is with what follows. No doubt we may infer that he had a splendid funeral; this splendid carrying to the grave is for him what the carrying into Abraham's bosom was for Lazarus,—it is his equivalent. But his death is for him an awakening from his flattering dream of ease and pleasure upon the stern and terrible realities of the life to come. He has sought to save his life, and has lost it. The play, in which he has acted the rich man, is ended, and as he goes off the stage, he is stripped bare of all the trappings with which he has been furnished in order to sustain his "part;" all that remains is the fact that he has played it badly, and so will have extremest blame from Him who allotted him the character to sustain.[6]

From this verse, the scene of the parable passes into the unknown world of spirits, but He to whom both worlds are open and manifest speaks without astonishment, as of things which He knows. It is not easy now to separate between what is merely figure, vehicle for truth, and the essential truth itself. We may safely say that the form in which the expression of pain, and of desire after alleviation, embodies itself, is figurative, as is the dialogue between Dives and Abraham. It is indeed the hope and longing for deliverance which alternately rises, and is again crushed by the voice of the condemning law speaking in and through the conscience; as by the seeing of Lazarus in Abraham's bosom, we recognize the truth that the misery of the wicked will be heightened by the comparison which they will be continually making of their lost estate with the blessedness of the faithful.

But to return; he that had that gorgeous funeral, is now *in hell,* or rather, in Hades; for as *Abraham's bosom* is not heaven, though it will issue in heaven, so neither is Hades *hell,* though to issue in it, when death and Hades shall be cast into the lake of fire, which is the proper hell (Rev. xx. 14). It is the place of painful restraint, where the souls of the wicked are reserved to the judgment of the great day; it is "the deep" mentioned in Luke viii. 31,—for as that other blessed place has a foretaste of heaven, so has this place a foretaste of hell; Dives is *in torments,* his purple robe has become a garment of fire, as he himself says: *I am tormented in this flame.*

We can believe that for a while all may have seemed as a fearful dream. But when at length he had convinced himself it was no dream, but an awaking, and would take the measure of his actual condition, *he lifted up his eyes, and seeth Abraham afar off, and Lazarus in his bosom* (Isai. lxv. 13, 14). *And he cried and said, Father Abraham,* still clinging to the hope that his fleshly privileges will profit him something. But this, which was once his glory, is now the very stress of his guilt. That he, a son of Abraham, that man of princely heart, should have so denied through his life all which the name "son of Abraham" was meant to teach him, this it was which had brought him to that place. Nor does Abraham deny the relationship—*Son,* yet this, coupled as it was with the refusal of his request, rings the knell of his latest hope. Infinitely slight was the best alleviation he had looked for,—a drop of water on his fiery tongue! Nothing could have marked more strongly how far he has fallen, how conscious he has himself become of the depth of that fall. Augustine: "The proud man of time, the beggar of hell."

In this prayer of the rich man we have the only invocation of saints in Scripture, and certainly not a very encouraging one. He can speak of "father Abraham," and his "father's house," but he will know nothing of that other Father whom the Prodigal had found. For he is as far as heaven is from hell, from the faith of the prophet (Isai. lxiii. 16). And the pity which he refused to show, he fails to obtain. "He lacked the drop, who denied the crumb" (Augustine). He has not made friends of the mammon of unrighteousness, and now has none to receive him into everlasting habitations. It is clear that Abraham's reply is a refusal of his petition, but the exact meaning of the words, *Thou in thy lifetime receivedst thy good things,* is not so certain. There are two explanations,—the commonest one makes *thy good things* to signify temporal felicities. "Son, thou hadst thy choice, the things temporal, or the things eternal, thou didst choose those; and now it is idle to think of altering thy choice." The other explanation would make *thy good things* to be good actions or good qualities. In the words of Bishop Sanderson, it was as if Abraham had said, "If thou hadst anything good in thee, remember thou hast had thy reward in earth already, and now there remaineth nothing but the full punishment of thine ungodliness in hell; but as for Lazarus, he hath had the chastisement of his infirmities [his *evil things*] on earth already, and now remaineth for him nothing but the full rewards (through grace) of his godliness, in heaven." This was the view of Chrysostom, as also of Gregory the Great, and it has certainly something to commend it.

But however this may be, there is this meaning in the passage, which is found so often in Scripture, namely, that a course of unbroken prosperity is ever an augury of ultimate reprobation (Ps. xvii. 14; Luke vi. 24, 25). If the dross which is in every man be not purged out by the fire of affliction, he cannot be a partaker of holiness. Such was the experience of Dives.[7] Moreover, besides that law of retaliation, requiring that the unmerciful should not receive mercy, the fact is brought home to Dives, that with death begins the separation of the elements of good and evil, which elements in this world are mingled. Good is gathered to good, and evil to evil,—and this separation is permanent. *Between us and you there is a great gulf fixed,*[8] a yawning chasm, too deep to be filled up, and too wide to be bridged over; *so that they who would pass from hence to you cannot, neither can they pass to us that would come from thence.* Of course the desire of passing thither cannot be for the purpose of changing their condition; but they cannot pass, he would say, even to yield a momen's comfort to any who are in that place.

But though repulsed for himself, he has a request to urge for others. *I pray thee, therefore, father, that thou wouldest send him to my father's house, for I have five brethren, that he may testify unto them, lest they also come into this place of torment.* Lazarus will be able to *testify* to the reality of that unseen world at which he and his brothers perhaps had mocked together. In this anxiety for his brethren's good, some have found the proof that suffering was already doing its work by awakening within him the slumbering germ of good; and with this view, would of necessity be connected his own ultimate restoration. But the request grows out of another root. There lies in it a secret justifying of himself, and accusing of God: "If only I had been sufficiently warned, if God had only given me clear evidences of the need of repentance, and of this place as the goal of a worldly life, I had never come hither. But at least, let my brethren be warned."

Abraham's answer is brief, and almost stern. "They *are* warned. *They have Moses and the prophets, let them hear them.*" Our Lord plainly indicated thus, that to hear Moses was to hear of life eternal and an after retribution (Matt. xxii. 31, 32). But he again cries: *Nay, father Abraham, but if one went unto them from the dead, they will repent.* The man's contempt of God's word, which he showed on earth, follows him beyond the grave. We have here, reappearing in hell, the "Show us a sign that we may believe," which was so often on the lips of the Pharisees on earth. But *if they hear not Moses and the prophets, neither will they be persuaded though one rose from the dead.*[9] These words demand care. Dives had said, *they will repent;* Abraham replies, they will not even *be persuaded.* Dives—*if one went unto them from the dead;* Abraham—No, not if *one rose from the dead.*

This reply of Abraham's is most weighty, as giving us an insight into the nature of faith, that it is a moral act; an act of the will and the affections as well as of the understanding; so that it cannot be forced by signs and miracles, for where there is a determined alienation of the will and affections from the truth, no impression made by these miracles, even if they be allowed to be genuine, will be more than transitory. Nor will there fail always to be a loophole somewhere, by which unbelief can escape; and this is well, or we should have in the Church the faith of devils, who believe and tremble. Compare the conduct of the Pharisees (John xi. 47; xii. 10). We see what multitudes acknowledge that the resurrection of Christ sets the seal to His claims, and yet are not brought at all nearer to repentance and faith. In exactly the spirit of Abraham's refusal, our Lord acted after His resurrection (Acts x. 41). This was a mercy as well as a judgment, for they would not have been persuaded even by one who rose from the dead.

It remains only to give a slight sketch of their interpretation, who maintain that this parable has also an allegorical meaning. Dives then represents the Jewish nation, clad in the purple of the king, and the fine linen of the priest. They were amply furnished with all spiritual blessings (Isai. v. 2, 4; Rom. ix. 4). But this talent of talents they turned into a selfish thing; Lazarus the beggar lay unrelieved at their gate, and without it, for the Gentiles were "aliens from the commonwealth of Israel,"—and full of sores. These sores of the Gentile world are enumerated in Rom. i. 23-32. That the beggar desired the crumbs of the rich man's table, has plainly a meaning. The yearning of the Gentiles after something better than aught they possessed, was, in fact, a yearning after that which the Jew had, and which, had he been faithful, he would have imparted.

The dying of Lazarus and his reception into Abraham's bosom are explained by 1 Pet. ii. 10—"which in time past were not a people, but are now the people of God . . . " (Eph. ii. 11-13). But Dives dies also,—the Jewish economy comes to an end, and now Dives is *in hell*. Who can read the history of the latter days of the Jewish nation, and not feel the force of this? Nay, and ever since have they not been *in torments?* In proof, turn to the word of prophecy (Lev. xxvi. 14-39; Deut. xxviii. 15-68), or call to mind our Lord's words (Luke xiii. 28-30). But as Dives looked for relief from Lazarus, so is the Jew look-ing for the alleviation of his miseries through some bettering of his outward estate,—some improvement of his civil condition, but which, if granted to him, would prove no more than a drop of water on the tongue. He knows not that it is the wrath of God which constitutes his misery.

By the five brethren of Dives will be set forth, according to this scheme, all who hereafter are tempted to the the same abuse of their spiritual privileges. When the Gentile Church sins as the Jewish Church did before it, glorying in its gifts rather than using them for others, contented to see in its very bosom a population outcast, save in name, from its privileges and blessings, and to see beyond its limits millions of heathens to whom it has but little care to impart the knowledge of Christ, then is it in danger, like the brethren of Dives, of coming with him to this place of torment.[10] So that the latter part of this parable speaks to us Gentiles, as Paul spoke to the Gentile converts at Rome; "Behold therefore the goodness and severity of God; on them which fell severity, but towards thee, goodness, if thou continue in His goodness; otherwise, thou also shalt be cut off" (Rom. xi. 22).

CHAPTER XXVII.

UNPROFITABLE SERVANTS

Luke xvii. 7-10.

SOME interpreters find a connection between this parable and the discourse which precedes it, while others affirm that none can be traced. Theophylact supposes, that in the sixth verse the Lord had declared how great things a living faith would enable His disciples to perform; but lest they should thereby fall into a snare of pride, He spoke this parable. Other expositors, seeking no connection, affirm that it merely teaches, in a general manner, how God is debtor to no man, that all we can do is of duty, and nothing of merit, and hence that deep humility becomes us.

Altogether different from these interpretations is that proposed by Grotius. According to this, the parable is made to represent the servile standing of the Jew under the old covenant. The arguments are mainly these: the common interpretation sets forth in a wrong aspect the relations between Christ and His people. Is it likely that He who said, "Henceforth I call you not servants, but I have called you friends," would bring forward in so strong a light, the service done to Him as one merely servile, and for which He would render them no thanks? Compare Luke xii. 37. On the other hand, the parable does, it is affirmed, exactly set forth the relation of the greater part of the Jews to God. To be sure, they did a certain work, but as it was without love and faith, they were *unprofitable servants,* in whom the Lord could take no pleasure.

There is something attractive in this exposition and it is worthy of respectful consideration. Yet the present parable need not be opposed to, but rather should be balanced with, that other saying of our Lord's (Luke xii. 37) above referred to. This is

173

the way God *might* deal; it is not said that He *will* deal in this way. This is the relation which, in strict justice, He might assume; the other is that which, according to the riches of His grace, He will assume. We are humbly to remember this. It is only to the humble, indeed, that He *can* give grace, for as it is certain that the unclean vessel will altogether taint the wine poured into it, so, without humility, the gifts of God will be perverted to spiritual wickedness, more deadly than the natural corruptions of the heart. Doubtless, the relation of the Christian to his Lord is set forth here under a somewhat severer aspect than is usual under the New Covenant. (Our translation makes it seem severer than it need; for the words, *Doth He thank that servant?* would be better, "Doth He count Himself especially beholden to that servant?") Yet the experience of every heart will bear witness that this side of the truth as well as the other, should be set forth,—that we should feel that a necessity is laid upon us,—that we are not to question our Master's will, but to do it. This fear does not exclude love, but is its true guardian; they mutually support one another: for while it is true that motives drawn from gratitude and love must ever be the chief incentives to obedience (Rom. xii. 1), yet so long as our hearts are not made perfect in love, we must be presented with others also. And while our Lord is graciously pleased to accept our work, and to reward it, we should ever be reminded that this is an act of His free grace; for there is another footing upon which it might be placed, that of the parable, upon which we ourselves must evermore put it.

A more real difficulty, as it appears to me, is this: that in the first part of the parable (ver. 7, 8) the purpose seems to be to commend patience in the Lord's work— that we do not, after we have made some exertion, account that we have a claim to be exempted henceforth from strenuous toil, but rather take example from the servant. But in the second part (vers. 9, 10), it is no longer this patient continuance in well-doing, but humility, that is enjoined—the confession that, at best, our service is poor and of little value. The solution is, however, I suppose, that impatience under deferred reward, with the desire to be released from labor, springs from over-estimation of our work; while he who feels that all which he has yet done is but little, as he will not think that he has a claim to a release from toil, so neither will he count that God is his debtor. The two wrong states of mind spring from the same root, and are to be met by the same remedy, namely, by our learning to know what our actual relation to God is,—that it is one of servants to a master.

With regard to the actual words of the parable, there is not much to remark. The waiting at the table with the dress girded was a mark of servitude. Note, then, the condescension of the Son of God, in His saying, Luke xii. 37, and in His doing, John xiii. 4. As to the confession which He puts into the mouths of His disciples, *When ye shall have done all these things which are commanded you, say, We are unprofitable servants*[1] (as many have observed before), if this they are to say when they have done all, how much more, when their consciences bear them witness, as his conscience must bear witness to every man, that they have grievously failed and come short of their duty.

CHAPTER XXVIII.

THE UNJUST JUDGE

Luke xviii. 1-8.

*H*E *spake a parable unto them,* the disciples,[1] *that men ought always to pray,* that men must *needs* pray always, if they would escape the things coming on the earth (see Luke xvii.). Not so much the duty, or the suitableness, as the absolute necessity of instant persevering prayer is here declared. In this precept to pray always (comp. Eph. vi. 18; 1 Thess. v. 17), there is nothing impossible commanded if we regard prayer as the continual desire of the soul after God,—having indeed its times of intensity, but not being confined to those times.[2] "That soul," says Donne, "that is accustomed to direct herself to God upon every occasion, that, whatsover string be stricken in her, base or treble, her high or her low estate, is ever turned towards God— that soul prays sometimes when it does not know that it prays."

None but the Son of God might have ventured to use the comparison of an *unrighteous* judge. We must not seek, as many have striven to do, to extenuate his unrighteousness; but on the contrary, the greater we conceive this to have been, the more does the encouraging truth come out which the Lord would enforce. If a bad man will yield to the mere force of the importunity which he hates, how much more certainly will a righteous God be prevailed on by the faithful prayer which He loves. This judge had reached that point of reckless wickedness, that he was alike indifferent to God and man.[3] The case, therefore, of any suppliant was the more hopeless, especially of one weak and poor. Such, no doubt, was the widow of the parable. Many writers have noticed the exceeding desolation of the state of widowhood in the East, and the consequent exposure to all manner of oppression; of this, the numerous warnings in Scripture against such oppression, are sufficient evidence (Exod. xxii. 22; Deut. xxiv. 17; Mal. iii. 5, and many more).

How fitly, then, does this widow represent the Church under that persecution which is always going forward.[4] Nor need we see in her only the Church at large, but also any single soul in conflict with the powers of darkness and the world. The adversary then (1 Pet. v. 8) is the prince of the darkness of this world. The elect are here represented as in conflict with those adverse powers, till under a sense of their helplessnss to affect their own deliverance, a cry is wrung out from them for aid; chiefly for that which shall be final and complete, at the revelation of the Son of Man in His glory. The words in which their need finds utterance, *Avenge me of mine adversary,* wonderfully express the relation in which we stand to the evil which, we are conscious, is mightily working within us,—that it is not our very self, but an alien power, holding us in bondage. It is one great work of the Spirit of God to make us feel this distinctness between us and the evil which is in us (Rom. vii.). The renewed man knows that he has an adversary, but for his comfort he knows also that this adversary is not his very self; and knowing this, he is able to cry, "Deliver me from the oppression of mine adversary." This is the same petition that we make daily, when we say, "Deliver us from evil," or rather "from the Evil One."[5]

For a time the judge was deaf to the widow's petition; *He would not for a while.* God often *seems to man* to be acting thus. And when His people receive no speedy answer, they are tempted to hard thoughts of God, and to say with the storm-tost disciples, "Carest thou not that we perish?" Now this parable is intended, in fact, to meet this very difficulty and temptation.—We have, in ver. 4, 5, recorded, not what was spoken aloud, but the voice of the heart, as that heart spake in the hearing of God. *He said within himself, Though I fear not God, nor regard man, yet because this widow troubleth me, I*

will avenge her, lest by her continual coming she weary me.[6]
Compare Matt. xv. 23; this parable and the miracle there
recorded, form altogether an interesting parallel. It is likely
that between the parable and its application,—between ver. 5
and 6,—the Lord paused awhile, and then again resumed; *Hear
what the unjust judge saith; and shall not God avenge His own
elect?* The righteous God is here opposed to the unrighteous
judge; the elect, the precious before God, to the widow, the
despised among men; their prayers, to her clamor; and the days
and nights during which those prayers are made, to the com-
paratively short time during which she beset the judge. The
certainty that the elect will be heard, rests not, however, on their
mighty and assiduous crying, as its ultimate ground, but on their
election by God, which is, therefore, here brought especially into
notice.[7] Shall He not avenge them, asks the Lord, *though He
bear long with them?* or since that phrase is mostly used in
Scripture, to set forth the relation of God to the sins of men, it
would avoid perplexity if here we should use the phrase,
"though He bear them long in hand?" or, "though He delay
with them long?" that is, long, as men count length. In fact
He will avenge them speedily, delivering them from the furnace
of affliction the instant that patience has had its perfect work;
so that there is meant to be an apparent contradiction between
ver. 7 and that which follows, while there really is none. The
relief which to man's impatience seems to tarry long, in fact
arrives speedily; it could not, according to the far-seeing and
loving counsels of God, have arrived a moment earlier. We find
practical illustrations of these words in our Lord's conduct with
the family of Bethany (John xi. and see also Matt. xiv. 24, 25).
The point of the closing words, *Nevertheless, when the Son of
man cometh, shall He find faith*[8] *on the earth?* is not that there
will be at the last but few, if any, faithful; but that the faith even
of the faithful will be almost failing, so urgent will be the distress when He shall appear for salvation and deliverance. All

help will seem utterly to have failed, so that the Son of man will hardly find that faith which believes that light will break forth even when the darkness is thickest, and believing this, continues to pray.[9] The verse stands parallel to, and may be explained by, those other words of our Lord: "For the elect's sake," lest their faith also should fail, and so no flesh be saved, "those days shall be shortened" (Matt. xxiv. 22).

CHAPTER XXIX.

THE PHARISEE AND THE PUBLICAN

Luke xviii. 9-14.

THE last parable was to teach us that prayer must be earnest and persevering; this, that it must also be humble.[1] It was spoken *unto certain which trusted in themselves that they were righteous, and despised others.*

Two men went up into the temple to pray, we are to suppose at one of the fixed hours of devotion (Acts iii. 1) ;—the Pharisee, a specimen of those, who, satisfying themselves with a certain external freedom from gross offences, have remained ignorant of the plague of their own hearts; the Publican, the representative of all who, though they have grievously transgressed, are now heartily mourning for their sins, and yearning after one who shall deliver them from these, and from their penalty. To pray standing was the manner of the Jews (1 Kings viii. 22; 2 Chron. vi. 12; Matt. vi. 5) ; though in moments of a more than ordinary humiliation, they prostrated themselves (Dan. vi. 10; 2 Chron. vi. 13; Acts xxi. 5).

The Pharisee's prayer at first seems to promise well—*God, I thank thee,* yet its early promise quickly disappears; under pretended thankfulness self-exaltation is thinly veiled. He thanks God, indeed, but not aright; for the right recognition of God's grace will always be accompanied with deep self-abasement, while we confess our infinite shortcomings with such help at command; and moreover we shall thank Him as much for the sense of need which He has awakened within us, as for the supplies of grace which he has given us. But this Pharisee thanks God that He is *not as other men,* dividing the whole of mankind into two classes, he in the one class, all the world besides in the other. And as he can think nothing too good of himself, so

181

nothing too bad of them; they are *extortioners, unjust, adulterers.*
And then his eye alighting on the publican, of whom he may
have known nothing except that he was a publican, he drags
him into his prayer. *He,* thank God, has no need to beat his
breast, nor to cast his eyes in shame upon the ground.

So perfect is he in regard to the commands of the second table.
He now returns to the first. *I fast twice in the week.* According
to the law of Moses, but one fast-day in the year was appointed,
the great day of atonement (Lev. xvi. 29), but the more religious
Jews, and especially the Pharisees, kept two fasts weekly. Thus
does he; nor is this all: *I give tithes of all that I possess* (rather
of all that I *earn*). The law commanded only to tithe the fruit
of the field and produce of the cattle (Num. xviii. 21; Deut.
xiv. 22; Lev. xxvii. 30), but he tithed mint and cummin (Matt.
xxiii. 23),—all. He would, therefore, in both respects, lay claim
to doing more than might strictly be demanded of him; he
would bring in God as his debtor. Acknowledgment of wants
or confession of sins, there is none in his prayer, if prayer it can
be called.[2] Augustine—"Thou hast said that thou hast all, thou
hast asked for nothing;—in what respect, then, hast thou come
to *pray?*"

It aggravates our sense of the moral outrage involved in the
Pharisee's contemptuous allusion to his fellow-worshipper, if we
keep in mind that in this last we are to see one who at this
very moment was passing into the kingdom of God, one in
whom under sore pangs the new man was being born. For *the
publican standing afar off, would not lift up so much as his
eyes[3] unto heaven,* to the dwelling of the Holy One (Ezra ix. 6).
He stood *afar off,* not but that he had a full right to approach,
for undoubtedly he also was a Jew; but in reverent awe, not
presuming to press nearer to the holy place. Moreover, he *smote
upon his breast,* a sign of self-accusation, or inward grief, at the
same time *saying, God be merciful to me a sinner,* or "to me
the sinful one." The selection of the word here rendered "be

merciful," is very observable, for it implies not reconciliation merely, but reconciliation affected through some gift, or sacrifice, or offering. And as the other had singled himself out as the one holy one in the world, so the publican singles himself out as the chief of sinners—the man in whom all sins have met. Who at that moment when he is first truly convinced of his sins, thinks any other man's sins can be equal to his own?

And he found the mercy which he asked; his prayer ascended, a sacrifice of sweet savor, while the prayer of the other was blown back like smoke into his own eyes; *I tell you this man went down to his house justified rather than the other.* Not merely was he justified in the secret counsels of God, but a sweet sense of a received forgiveness was shed abroad upon his heart. The other meanwhile went down from the temple with the same cold, dead heart, with which he had gone up. Christ does not mean that one by comparison with the other was justified, for there are no degrees in justification, but that the one absolutely was justified, and the other was not;[4] so that here the words recorded in Ps. cxxxviii. 6; Isa. lvii. 15, have their fulfilment.

The whole parable fitly concludes with that weighty saying, *For every one that exalteth himself shall be abased, and he that humbleth himself shall be exalted.*

CHAPTER XXX.

THE POUNDS

Luke xix. 11-27.

MOST of what might be said upon this parable has been anticipated in that of the Talents. Each bears the most decisive marks of its adaptation to the peculiar circumstances under which each was spoken. *He added and spake a parable, because he was nigh to Jerusalem, and because they thought that the kingdom of God should immediately appear.* It was uttered, then, to teach the need of a patient waiting for Christ by His disciples; and not merely that, but also of an active working for Him during His absence. But He had also other hearers on this His last journey to Jerusalem—a multitude drawn together by curiosity, and by other mingled motives. These were liable to be drawn presently into the mighty stream of hostility which was running against Him. For them is meant that part of the parable recorded in ver. 14-27.

In the great Roman empire, such a circumstance as that which serves for the groundwork of this parable can have been of no infrequent occurrence.[1] That he who should thus seek and obtain a kingdom was a *nobleman,* is only what we should expect. And this has its deeper significance, for who was of such noble birth as He who, even according to the flesh, came of earth's first blood—was the Son of Abraham, the Son of David; who was, besides, the only-begotten Son of God?

This nobleman goes to receive, not a kingdom at a distance, but rather the investiture of that kingdom whereof he has hitherto been only one of the more illustrious citizens.[2] This is implied by the message of his fellow-citizens, *We will not have this man to reign over us.*[3] And Christ went, not only to be enthroned in His heavenly state, but also to receive solemn in-

185

vestiture of that earthly kingdom which hereafter He shall, returning, claim as His own.

Before he went, however, *he called his ten servants,* or rather ten servants of his, *and delivered them ten pounds, and said unto them, Occupy*[4] *till I come.* A pound (mina) is equal to £4 1s. 3d. In St. Matthew, talents (a talent = £243 15s.) were given, for that parable was to the apostles. How remarkable are these occupations of peace in which they should be engaged, and that too, while a rebellion was going on. Men, feeling strongly, have supposed that the kingdom of God was immediately to appear (ver. 11), and that they, and not Christ Himself, were to bring it into its outward form and subsistence—instead of seeing that their part was, with the silent occupation of their talent, to prepare the world for the coming of that kingdom, which should take place on the return of the King in His glory.

The Jews were especially Christ's fellow-*citizens,* for, according to the flesh, He was of the seed of Abraham; and they hated Him not merely in His life, but every persecution of His servants was a message of defiance sent after Him, *We will not have this man reign over us.* And Theophylact well observes, how twice this very declaration found formal utterance from their lips— once when they cried to Pilate, "We have no king but Cæsar;" and again when they said, "Write not, the King of the Jews." If we find the full accomplishment of all which this parable contains, not at the destruction of Jerusalem, but at the day of judgment, then these rebellious citizens will be not merely the Jews, but all such evil men as by word or deed openly deny their relation and subjection to Jesus, as their Lord and King,[5] and their message will have its entire fulfilment in the great apostacy of the last days, which shall be a speaking of great things against Him (Rev. xiii. 5, 6; Dan. vii. 25).

On the following verses (15—23) there is little to say which has not been said elsewhere. The rewards which the nobleman imparts to his faithful servants are royal: he sets them over cities.6 This method of showing grace to servants was not uncommon in the East. The rewards, too, are proportioned to their fidelity. Those who stand by, and are bidden to take the pound from the slothful servant,7 and give it to the ablest, are clearly the angels, who never fail to take an active part in all scenes descriptive of the final judgment.

When the king has thus distributed rewards and penalties to those of his own household—for the Church is the household of God—he proceeds to execute vengeance on all who had openly cast off allegiance to him (Prov. xx. 8). They are slain before his face; as their guilt was greater, so their punishment is more terrible, than that of the slothful servant. The slaying of the king's enemies *in his presence* belongs to the innermost kernel of the parable. The words set forth fearfully the unmitigated wrath of the Lord Jesus against His enemies—*His* enemies only as they are the enemies of all righteousness—which shall be revealed at the last (Rev. xiv. 10).8 We may compare Heb. i. 13, and we can learn from Josh. x. 24, what the image is, that underlies that passage.

NOTES

Introductory Remarks

CHAPTER I.

1. "A parable;" from the Greek *parabole,* which is from a verb signifying *to put forth one thing before* or *beside* another; and it is assumed, when *parabole* is used for parable, though not necessarily included in the word, that the purpose for which they are set side by side is that they may be compared one with the other.

Jerome finely calls a parable "a shadow, as it were, of truth, cast before."

2. "In this raillery the fabulist frequently indulges," as in La Fontaine's celebrated fable of The Ant and the Grasshopper, in which the ant, in reply to the petition of the grasshopper which is starving in the winter, reminds it how it sung all the summer.

CHAPTER II.

1. "The parabolical element of teaching." There is a natural delight in this, which has impressed itself upon our language. To *like* a thing is to compare it to some other thing, from which process arises a pleasurable emotion. That we *like* what is *like,* is the explanation of the pleasure which rhymes give us.

CHAPTER III.

1. The Gnostics. Irenæus likens their dealings with Scripture to their fraud who should break up some work of exquisite mosaic, bearing the likeness of a king, and then so recompose the pieces as to express the image of a dog or fox, hoping that, since they could point to the stones as the same, they should be able to persuade the simple that this was the king's likeness still. The miracles were submitted by them to the same process of interpretation.

2. The Cathari and Bogomili. They made the servant that owed the ten thousand talents to be Satan, the servant's wife his intelligence, the children the angels subject to him. God pitied him, and did not take from him his higher intelligence, his subjects or his goods; he promising, if God would be patient with him, to create men enough to fill the fallen angels' place.

Parables

CHAPTER I.

1. The sea of Galilee. The Jewish writers would have it that it was beloved by God above all the waters of Canaan; and because of the beauty and rich fertility of its banks, its name Genesareth has been sometimes derived, which some interpret "the garden of riches," though the derivation, I believe, is insecure. Josephus rises into high poetical animation while he is describing its attractions. Robinson *(Bibl. Researches)* gives a

191

far less enthusiastic account; when he visited it, the verdure of the spring had disappeared.

2. As it belongs to the essentially popular nature of the Gospels that parables should be found in them rather than in the Epistles, where indeed they never appear, so it belongs to the popular character of the parable that it should thus rest upon the familiar doings of common life; while at the same time the Lord, using these to set forth eternal and spiritual truths, ennobles them, showing, as He does, how they continually reveal the deepest mysteries of His kingdom. What a dignity and significance have these few words ("a sower went forth to sow") given in all after times to the toils of the husbandman.

Salmeron, very beautifully: "As Christ is Physician and medicine, Priest and victim, Redeemer and redemption, Lawmaker and law, Doorkeeper and door, so Sower and seed. For the Gospel itself is nothing else than Christ incarnate, born, preaching, dying, rising, sending the Holy Spirit, collecting the Church, and sanctifying and guiding it."

3. "Hard as a pavement." H. de Sto. Victore: "The 'way' is the heart worn down and made barren by the constant passage of evil thoughts."

4. *When the sun was up* . . . Generally the light and warmth of the sun set forth the genial and comfortable workings of God's grace, as eminently Mal. iv. 2; but not always, for see, besides the passage before us, Ps. cxxi. 6; Isa. xlix. 10; Rev. vii. 16. Bede: "Those are hearts which, for the hour, are delighted with the sweetness only of the discourse they have heard, and with its heavenly promises."

5. *Root in himself*. With allusion to this passage, the Greek Fathers call men of faith *deep-rooted*, and *many-rooted*.

6. *Tribulation*. This word rests upon the idea of sifting—*tribulatio* from *tribulum*, the threshing-roller, and thus used to signify those afflictive processes by which in the moral discipline of men, God separates their good from their evil, their wheat from their chaff.

7. *Choked it*. The image of an evil growth strangling a nobler is permanently embodied in our language in *cockle*, a well known weed, a word derived from the Anglo-Saxon, *ceocan*, to choke.

It is evident that, in the great symbolic language of the outward world, *thorns* have a peculiar fitness to express influences hostile to the truth, themselves the consequences and evidences of sin, of a curse which has passed on from man to earth (Gen. iii. 17, 18), till that earth had none other but a *thorn*-crown to yield to its Lord.

8. It may seem strange at first sight that cares and pleasures, which appear so opposite to one another, should here be linked together, and have the same evil consequences attributed to them; but the Lord does in fact here present earthly life on its two sides — its crushing, oppressive side, the poor man's toil how to live at all, and its flattering side.

9. How can any heart be called *good*, before the Lord and the Spirit have made it so? Augustine asks: "What is this? whose were the good works?" and answers: "The beginning of good works is the confession of evil works. Thou doest truth, how? thou dost not flatter thyself, dost not say, I am righteous, when thou art wicked; and thou beginnest to do truth."—As our Saviour in this parable, so the Jewish doctors divide hearers of the words of wisdom into four classes. The best they liken to

a sponge, that drinks in all it receives, and again expresses it to others; the worst to a strainer, that retains only the dregs, or to a sieve, that retains only the bran.

CHAPTER II.

1. *The Son of man.* Our Lord was often understood, in the early Church and among the Reformers, by this title to signify nothing more than His participation in the human nature; while others have said that He assumed the name as the one by which the hoped-for Messiah was already commonly known among the people. But it is clear that, on the contrary, the name was a strange one to them; compare John xii. 34. The popular name for the Messiah, when Christ came, was, Son of David (Matt. ix. 27; xii. 23; xv. 22; xx. 31, etc). No doubt He claimed the title (already given Him in the Old Test. Dan. vii. 13), inasmuch as it was He who alone realized the idea of man, the one true and perfect flower which had ever unfolded itself out of the root and stalk of humanity.

2. *The field is the world.* Words few and slight, a great battle has been fought over them, greater perhaps than over any single phrase in the Scripture, if we except the consecrating words of the Eucharist. Aside from the merely personal question concerning the irregularity of certain ordinations, the grounds on which the Donatists justified their separation from the Church Catholic were these: The idea of the Church, they said, is that of a perfectly holy body; holiness is not merely one of its essential predicates, but *the* essential, to which all others must be subordinated. They did not deny that it was possible that hypocrites might be concealed in its bosom, but where the evidently ungodly were suffered to remain in communion with it, not separated off by the exercise of discipline, then it forfeited the character of the true Church, and the faithful were to come out from it; else, they would themselves be defiled. In support of this view, they maintained that such passages as Isa. lii. 1, and all others which spoke of the future freedom of the Church from evil, were meant to be applicable to it in its present condition, and consequently, where they were not applicable, there could not be the Church. Here, as on so many other points, the Church owes to Augustine, not the forming of her doctrine, for that she owes to no man, but the bringing out into her clear consciousness that which hitherto she had indeed possessed, yet had not worked out into a perfect clearness, even for herself. By him she replied, not in any way gainsaying the truth which the Donatists proclaimed, that holiness must be an essential predicate of the Church, but only refusing to accept their idea of that holiness, and showing how in the Church, which they had forsaken, this quality was to be found, and combined with other as essential qualities.

The Church Catholic, he affirmed, despite all appearances to the contrary, *is* a holy body, for they only are its members who are in true and living fellowship with Christ, therefore partakers of His sanctifying Spirit. All others, however they may have the outward notes of belonging to it, are *in* it, but not *of* it; they *press* upon Christ, like the thronging multitude; they do not *touch* Him, like the believing woman (Luke viii. 45). There are certain outward conditions, without which one cannot pertain to His Church, but with which one does not necessarily do so. And they who are thus in it, but not of it, whether hypocrites lying hid, or open offenders, who, from their numbers, may not without greater evils be expelled, do not defile the true members so long as these share not in their spirit, nor communicate with their evil deeds.

The Donatists wished to make the Church in its visible form and historic manifestation identical and co-extensive with the true Church which the Lord knoweth, and not man. Augustine also affirmed the identity of the Church now existing with the final and glorious Church; but he denied that they were co-extensive. He laid especial stress upon the fact that the Lord Himself had not contemplated His Church in its present state as perfectly free from evil. In proof, he appealed to this parable and that of the Draw-net, and not merely as stating historic fact —he urged also that all attempts to have it otherwise are here expressly forbidden.

We shall see hereafter how the Donatists sought to escape the argument drawn from the other parable. To this, they made answer:— "By the Lord's own showing, *the field* is not the Church, but the world. The parable, therefore, does not bear on the dispute betwixt us and you in the least." But it must be evident to every one not warped by a dogmatic interest, that the parable is, as the Lord announces at its first utterance, concerning the kingdom of heaven, or the Church. (Calvin: "Although Christ adds that the field is the world, yet it is not doubtful that He wished to apply this name to the Church in particular, concerning which He had begun His discourse. But since He was about to draw His plough promiscuously through all regions of the world, so that He might cultivate for Himself fields everywhere, and scatter the seed of life, He transferred *by synecdoche* to the world what fitted a part only.") It required no especial teaching to acquaint the disciples that in the *world* there would ever be a mixture of good and bad, though they must have been so little prepared to expect the same in the Church, that it was very needful to warn them beforehand, both that they might not be stumbled, and that they might know how to conduct themselves.

3. "Evil," not a generation, but a degeneration; as Augustine often expresses it, it has not an efficient but only a *de*-ficient cause.

4. *Let both grow together until the harvest.* The visible Church is to have its intermixture of good and bad until the end of time, and by consequence the fact of the bad being found mingled with the good will in no wise justify a separation from it, or an attempt to set up a little Church of our own. Where men will attempt this, besides the guilt of transgressing a plain command, it is not difficult to see what fatal effects on their own spiritual life it must have, what darkness it must bring upon them, and into what a snare of pride it must cast them. Thus Augustine often appeals to the fact that the Donatists had not succeeded, that they themselves would not dare to assert that they had succeeded, in forming what should even externally appear a pure communion; and since by their own acknowlegment there might be, and probably were, hypocrites and concealed ungodly among themselves, this was enough to render all such passages as Isa. lii. 1, as inapplicable to them as to the Church in its present condition.

Every young Christian in the time of his first zeal is tempted to be somewhat of a Donatist in spirit. Nay, it would argue little love or holy earnestness in him, if he had not this longing to see the Church of his Saviour a glorious Church without spot or wrinkle. But he must learn that the desire, righteous and holy as in itself, yet it is not to find its fulfilment in this present evil time; that on the contrary, the suffering from false brethren is one of the pressures upon him, which is meant to wring out from him a more earnest prayer that the Kingdom of God may appear.

Calvin's words are excellent: "There is this dangerous temptation, to think that there is no Church where complete purity may not appear. For whosoever may be carried away with this, it will at last be inevitable, that having separated from everybody else, he shall seem to himself the only holy person in the world, or in company with a few hypocrites set up a sect of his own. Why then did Paul recognize the Church of God in Corinth? Because he saw among them, Gospel-doctrine, Baptism, the Lord's Supper, by which marks merely a Church should be judged."

The harvest. Bishop Horsley distinguishes between the vintage and the harvest, which are the two images under which the consummation is so commonly represented. "The vintage is always an image of the season of judgment, but the harvest of the ingathering of the objects of God's final mercy. I am not aware that a single unexceptionable instance is to be found, in which the harvest is a type of judgment. In Rev. xiv. 15, 16, the sickle is thrust into the ripe harvest, and the earth is reaped, *i.e.,* the elect are gathered from the four winds of heaven. After this reaping of the earth the sickle is applied to the clusters of the vine, and they are cast into the great winepress of the wrath of God (ver. 18-20). In Joel iii. 13, the ripe harvest is the harvest of the vine, *i. e.,* the grapes fit for gathering, as appears by the context. In Jer. li. 33, the act of threshing out the harvest is the image of judgment. It is true the burning of the tares in Matt. xiii. is a work of judgment; but it is an accidental adjunct of the business, not the harvest itself." It may be a question whether the manner in which he makes our parable fit into his scheme is quite satisfactory.

5. *Then shall the righteous shine forth.* Full force is to be given to *forth.* Calvin: "It is a very great comfort that the sons of God, who now are either lying covered with squalor, or are hidden and unesteemed, or are even buried under reproaches, shall then, as in a clear sky and with every cloud dissipated, at once shine out brightly." Using a different image, Augustine says of the Christian as he is now—"His glory is hidden; when the Lord shall have come, then will it appear. For he flourishes, but as yet in winter; the root flourishes, but the branches are as if withered. Within is the pith which is flourishing, within are leaves, within is fruit; but they await the summer."

CHAPTER IV.

1. "There is no need, then . . . " The devil is "a roaring lion, seeking whom he may devour" (1 Pet. v. 8), yet this does not hinder the same title from being applied to Christ, "the lion of the tribe of Judah" (Rev. v. 5). Nor is it to be forgotten that if, on one side, the effects of

leaven on meal present an analogy to something evil in the spiritual world, they do also, on the other, to something good, as it is universally agreed that its effects on bread are to render it more tasteful, lighter, and more nourishing, and generally more wholesome.

Is it only a part of the suitable machinery of the parable, that the act of kneading being proper to women, it is *a woman* here who takes the leaven and puts it in the meal? or may we look for something more? Luke xv. 8 may suggest that the Holy Spirit is here meant. If it be asked, why as a woman? it may be replied, that the Spirit's organ is the Church. Again, why *three* measures of meal? Perhaps, because that was a common amount to mix at one time (Gen. xviii. 6). Yet it may be that it means something more. Some perceive in it illusion to the spread of the Gospel through the three parts of the then known world; some, like Jerome and Ambrose, find in it a pledge of the sanctification of body, soul, and spirit.

2. "A new power brought from above." Augustine, in whose time the fading away of all the glory of the ancient world was daily becoming more apparent, loved to contemplate the coming of Christ as a new and quickening power cast into the midst of an old and dying world, by the help of which the world might renew its youth.

CHAPTER V.

1. "Some draw a distinction between the field and the treasure; making the first to be the Scriptures, the second the knowledge of Christ:" so Augustine and Jerome.

2. *Selleth all that he hath, and buyeth this field.* The Lord is in fact exhorting to this in Matt. x. 37-39. And yet it is not merely a command. The dead leaves easily and as of themselves fall off from the tree, when propelled by the new blossoms and buds which are forcing their way from behind.

"Some have found a difficulty . . . " In books of casuistry, where they treat of the question how far and when a finder has a right to appropriate things found, this parable is frequently adduced. Apollonius of Tyana, being called in to decide a quarrel between the buyer and seller of such a field, adjudged it to whichever of the parties should be found, on scrutiny, to have lived the holiest life.

CHAPTER VI.

1. "The great Eureka breaks forth from his lips." Augustine: "Lord, Thou hast made us *for* Thee, and our heart is disquieted till it reacheth *to* Thee."

CHAPTER VII.

1. Much of what has been already said in considering the Tares will apply here. The same use has been made of either parable; there is the same continual appeal to this as to that in the Donatist controversy, and this conveys to all ages the same instruction as that. The minutes of the conference at Carthage show how the Donatists sought to evade the forces of the arguments drawn from this parable. They did not deny that Christ spoke, in this parable, of sinners being found mingled with the righteous in the Church, yet it was only *concealed* sinners, "since

the fishermen do not know what is in the net, placed as it is in the sea, until it is brought to the shore"; taking refuge in an accidental circumstance in the parable, viz., that so long as the nets are under water their contents cannot be seen.

2. *The angels shall come forth.* Everywhere in the Scripture we find the angels distinctly named as the executioners of the final separtation (Matt. xiii. 41; xxiv. 31; xxv. 31; Rev. xiv. 18, 19). Moreover, in each of the other parables of judgment, there is a marked distinction, which it is little likely should have been here renounced, between the present ministers of the kingdom and the future executors of doom —in the Tares, between the servants and the reapers, in the Marriage of the King's Son (Matt. xxii.) between the servants *(douloi)* and attendants *(diakonoi)*, in the Pounds (Luke xix.) between the servants and those that stand by.

3. "The seven parables related in this chapter . . ." The mystical number seven has offered to many interpreters a temptation too strong to be resisted for seeking in them some hidden mystery; and when the seven petitions of the Lord's prayer, and the names of the seven original deacons (Acts vi. 5.) have been turned into prophecy of seven successive states of the Church, not to speak of the seven Apocalyptic Epistles (Rev. ii. iii.), it was scarcely to be expected that these seven parables should have escaped being made prophetic of the same. Bengel applies the first parable to the times of Christ and His Apostles—the original period of sowing; the second (the Tares), to the age immediately following, when heresies began to abound; the third (the Mustard Seed), to the time of Constantine, when the Church evidently *gave* support, and furnished protection to the great ones of earth; the fourth (the Leaven), to the propagation of true religion through the whole world; the Hid Treasure, to the more hidden state of the Church signified in Rev. xii. 6; the Pearl, to the time when the kingdom shall be esteemed above all things, Satan being bound; while the Draw-Net details the ultimate confusion, separation, and judgment.

CHAPTER VIII.

1. There is nothing in the discourse going before, to lead immediately to Peter's question, to which this parable is an answer; and yet the words "*Then* came Peter," seem to make an unbroken connection. Perhaps it is thus: Peter must have felt in his Lord's injunctions concerning an offending brother (ver. 15-17), that the forgiveness of his fault was necessarily implied as having already taken place; since, till we had forgiven, we would not be in the condition to deal with him thus, for this dealing, even to the exclusion of him from Church-fellowship, is entirely a dealing in love (2 Thes. iii. 14, 15), and with a view to his recovery.

The command, in ver. 22, to forgive till seventy times seven, does not exclude a dealing, if need be, of severity, provided always it be a dealing in love. Our Lord's seventy times seven makes a wonderful contrast with Lamech's, the antediluvian Antichrist's, seventy and sevenfold of revenge (Gen. iv. 24).

2. "Peter's consciousness of this new law of love," that it was a law larger, more long-suffering, than the old; but there were yet deeper motives for his selection of the number seven. It is the number in the divine law with which the idea of remission was ever linked. The seven times seventh year was the year of jubilee (Lev. xxv. 28; comp. iv. 6, 17; xvi. 14, 15). Gregory of Nyssa suggests also the fact of the Sabbath being the seventh day.

3. *Ten thousand talents.* The sum here is immense, whatever talents we suppose these to have been, though it would differ very much in amount according to the talent which we assumed. According to Plutarch, it was exactly this sum of ten thousand talents with which Darius sought to buy off Alexander. We have some almost incredible notices of the quantities of gold in the East. Perchance the immensity of the sum may partly have moved Origen to his supposition, that it can only have been the Man of Sin that is here indicated, or stranger still, the Devil!

4. "A part of his property;" so, according to Roman law.

5. "It is because we go out . . ." Theophylact: "For no one abiding in God is without sympathy."

6. "How little man can offend against his brother, compared . . ." The Hebrew talent—300 shekels (Exod. xxxviii. 25, 26). Assuming this, the proportion of the two debts would be:

10,000 talents: 100 pence : : 1,250,000: 1, that is, one million two hundred and fifty thousand to one.

CHAPTER IX.

1. "For we cannot imagine . . ."—not even here in our present imperfect state, and much less in the perfected kingdom hereafter, for love "rejoices in the truth." Leighton: "Envy is without the divine choir, but the most absolute charity, by which each one, at the same time with his own, enjoys likewise the happiness of another, and is blessed, rejoicing in that indeed as if it were his own; whence there is amongst them a certain rebound and multiplication of blessedness; such as would be the splendor of a hall glittering with gold and gems, with a full circle of kings and magnates, whose walls should be covered on every side with the most brilliant mirrors.'

2. "At nine . . ." These would not, except just at the equinoxes, be exactly the hours, for the Jews, as well as the Greeks and Romans, divided the natural day, that between sunrise and sunset, into twelve equal parts (John xi. 9), which parts must of course have been considerably longer in summer than in winter. The longest day is a little more than fourteen hours, the shortest a little less than ten hours; an hour on the longest day was exactly twenty-two minutes longer than an hour on the shortest. Probably the day was also divided into four larger parts here indicated.

3. "Still one would not deny . . ." For in truth time belongs not to the kingdom of God. Not "How much hast thou done?" but "What art thou now?" will be the great question of the last day. Of course we must never forget that all which men have *done* will greatly affect what they *are;* yet still the parable is a protest against the Romanist's estimate of men's works, against all which would make the works the

end, and man the means, instead of man the end, and the works the means — against that scheme which, however unconsciously, lies at the root of so many of the confusions in our theology at this day.

This mechanical, as opposed to the dynamic idea of righteousness, is carried to the greatest perfection of all in the Chinese theology. Thus in that remarkable *Livre des recompenses et des peines,* the mechanic, or to speak more truly, the arithmetic idea of righteousness comes out with all possible distinctness; for example: "To become immortal, one must have amassed three thousand merits and eight hundred virtuous actions." How glorious, on the other hand, are Thauler's words upon the way in which we may have restored to us "the years which the canker-worm has eaten" (Joel ii. 25): "Let each one turn himself with all his powers highest and lowest away from every circumstance of place and time, and betake himself into that Now of eternity, where God essentially exists in a certain immovable Now. There, there is nothing past or future. There, the beginning and end of universal time are alike present. There, in God namely, all lost things are found, and they who are accustomed to betake themselves to God and abide in Him, become exceeding rich, nay, they find more than it is possible to lose."—It may be securely inferred that all between the last and the first hired received the penny as well; though it is the case of the first hired alone which is brought forward, as that in which the injustice, as the others conceived it, appeared the most striking. To assume, as so many have done, *e. g.* Olshausen, that these first hired had been doing their work negligently by comparison, is to assume that of which there is not the slightest trace in the narrative, and which morever effectually blunts the point of the parable—brings us back to the level of debt instead of grace from which to raise us the parable was expressly spoken. Singularly enough, exactly such a Jewish parable is to be found in the Talmud: "To what was R. Bon Bar Chaija like? To a king who hired many laborers, among whom there was one hired, who performed his task extraordinarily well. . . And the laborers murmured, saying 'We have labored hard all the day, and this man only two hours, yet he hath received as much wages as we.' The king said to them, 'He hath labored more in those two hours than you in the whole day.' So R. Bon plied the law more in eight and twenty years than another in a hundred years."

Josephus (*Antiquities,* 20, 9, 7) expressly says that Ananus (the Annas of the New Test.) paid the workmen who were employed in rebuilding or beautifying the temple a whole day's pay, *even though they should have labored but a single hour.*

4. "A penny." A denarius, a Roman silver coin. It was equal to about 16 or 17 cts., at the latter end of the commonwealth; afterwards, something less. It was not an uncommon, though a liberal day's pay. Morier mentions having noticed in the market-place at Hamadan (Persia) a custom like that alluded to in the parable: "Here we observed every morning before the sun rose, that a numerous band of peasants were collected with spades in their hands, waiting to be hired for the day to work in the surrounding fields. This custom struck me as a most

happy illustration of our Saviour's parable, particularly when, passing by the same place late in the day, we found others standing idle, and remembered His words, 'Why stand ye here all the day idle?' as most applicable to their situation, for on putting the very same question to them they answered us, 'Because no man hath hired us.' "

5. "The penny is to each what he would make it." Bellarmine: "The penny signifies eternal life; but as the same sun is seen more clearly by the eagle than by other birds, and the same fire warms those near to it more than those far off, so in the same eternal life one will see more clearly and enjoy more fully than another."

6. "*Just* to you and *good* to them." Comp. Rom. v. 7 ("righteous" and "good"), which is only to be explained by keeping fast hold of the opposition between the words.

7. The "reward" *has* relation to the work, but we receive a reward because God has promised it, not because we earn it.

CHAPTER XI.

1. "The image . . ." (See Isa. v. 1-7.) No doubt our Lord here takes up the prophecy there, the more willingly building on the old foundations, that His adversaries accused Him of destroying the law; and not in word only, but by the whole structure of the parable, connecting His own appearance with all that had gone before in Jewish history, so that men should look at it as the crowning and final act of that great dealing of mercy and judgment which had ever been going forward.

Bernard, comparing the Church to the vineyard, says: "Planted in faith, it sends out roots in charity, is dug about by the hoe of discipline, manured with the tears of the penitent, watered by the words of preachers, and so truly abounds in wine etc.; this wine, of a truth, maketh glad the heart of man, and the angels drink it with joy!" It no doubt belongs to the fitness of the image that a vineyard, if it is to bring forth richly, requires the *most* diligent and unceasing care, that there is no season in the year in which much has not to be done in it.

The vine-stock often appears on the Maccabaean coins as the emblem of Palestine; sometimes, too, the bunch of grapes and the vine-leaf.

2. "Nothing more . . ." Generally the wine-press is taken to signify the prophetic institution; thus, Irenaeus, Hilary, Ambrose. But all the explanations that are given appear fanciful.

"The vineyard itself will signify . . . ; and the husbandman may be compared to the priests . . ." A friend adds a note which I am sure every reader will be glad I have preserved: "I do not absolutely question the truth of this interpretation; but it seems to me rather an escape from a difficulty which does not exist more in the parable than in all our customary language about the Church. The Church is both *teacher* and *taught*; but the teachers are not merely the ministers: the whole Church of one generation teaches the whole Church of another, by its history, acts, words, mistakes . . ."

3. *His Son*, or as St. Mark has it, *One Son, His well-beloved.* This description marks as strongly as possible the dignity of Christ's person, and undoubtedly our Lord's hearers quite understood what He

meant. This has been often observed by the early Church writers, when proving the divinity of the Son.

4. *The heir.* Christ is "heir of all things" (Heb. i. 2), not as He is the Son of God, for there have always been Arian tendencies lurking in that interpretation, but as He is the Son of man.

May we not see in the thought of killing the heir and seizing on the inheritance, an allusion to the principle of all self-righteousness, which is a seizing on the Divine inheritance, a seeking to take down into self that light which is only light while it is recognized as something above self?

5. "Having thus prophesied . . ." We have a remarkable example of a like prophesying to men their wickedness, as a last endeavor to turn them from that wickedness, in 2 Kings viii. 12-15.

6. "God will deal with nations . . ." Unless this were so [*i. e.,* that nations have a living unity in themselves], all confession of our fathers' sin would be mere mockery, and such passages as Matt. xxiii. 32-35 without any meaning at all. This is one of the many ways in which God encounters our selfish, self-isolating tendencies.

CHAPTER XII.

1. The chief priests and scribes would have laid hands on Christ at the close of the foregoing parable, but for their fear of the people. Yet not even so did He give them up; but as He had set forth their relation to God as a relation of duty, so in this parable of the marriage of the King's Son He sets it forth in a more inviting light as a relation of privilege.

2. "The two favorite images—a marriage festival here." Vitringa: "The marriage symbolizes the very intimate union of Christ with the Church; the nuptial banquet shadows forth the blessings of grace, communion in those blessings, joy, and festivity."

3. "The dangers of *having a*nd of *getting* . . ." Comp. Luke xiv. 18, 19, where the guest who has bought a property and must needs go and see it, corresponds to the landed proprietor here—is one who would *enjoy* what he already possesses; and the guest who would fain try his five yoke of oxen, corresponds to the merchant here—being one who would *acquire* what as yet is his only in anticipation.

4. "May we not presume . . ." Often in the East a feast would have a great political significance, would in fact be a great gathering of the vassals of the king; contemplated on this side, their refusal to come at once assumes the aspect of rebellion. Thus there are many reasons for supposing that the feast recorded in Esth. i., is the same as the great gathering which Xerxes (Ahasuerus) made when he was planning his Greek expedition.

5. "The natural eyes sees only one . . ." Comp. 1 Chr. xxi. 16; the multitude beheld only the outward calamity, the pestilence, but David, with purged spiritual eye, saw the angel.

6. *The highways.* We must not permit this English expression to make us think of places in the country; the image throughout the parable is of a city.

7. "If the gift . . . , a contempt of the giver." We are not without example in the modern history of the East, of a vizier having lost his life, through this very failing to wear a garment of honor sent to him by the king. Olearius says, in describing an invitation to the table of the Persian king: "It was told us by the mehmandar, that we, according to their usage, must hang the plendid vests that were sent us from the king over our dresses, and so appear in his presence. The ambassadors at first refused; but it was urged so earnestly, the mehmandar alleging that the omission would greatly displease the king, that they finally consented, and hanged, as did we also, the splendid vests over their shoulders, and so the cavalcade proceeded." This passage is of value also as it clears away any difficulty which might have occurred to any from the apparent unfitness of the king's palace as a place for changing of apparel; in fact, there was no change of apparel, for the garment of honor was either a vest drawn over the other garments, or a mantle hung on the shoulders.

The Jews have a curious tradition about Esau, that he will be such a guest thrust out from the kingdom of God. "Esau the wicked will veil himself with his mantle, and sit among the righteous in Paradise; and the holy blessed God will draw and bring him out from thence, which is the sense of those words, Obad. 4, 6." (Jerusalem Talmud.)

8. "It has been abundantly disputed . . ." The Romanists have been eager to press this passage into their service. But when they assert that it must have been charity in which this guest was deficient, and not faith—for that he had faith, since he would not have been present at the feast at all unless externally a believer—they are merely taking advantage of the double meaning of the word faith, and playing off the occasional use of it as a bare assent to the truth against St. Paul's far deeper use of the word; and this most unfairly, for only in this latter sense would any attribute the exclusion to want of faith. Were it needful to decide absolutely for one or the other interpretation, I would far sooner accept the Reformers', for the flower may be said to be contained in the root, but not the root in the flower, and so charity in faith, but not faith in charity.

CHAPTER XIII.

1. Tertullian mentions an abuse which some of the Gnostics made of this parable: "The five foolish virgins are the five senses; foolish, inasmuch as they are easily deceived, and often give fallacious notices, while the five wise are the reasonable powers, which have the capability of apprehending ideas."

2. *Wise and foolish,* rather than *good* and *bad,* just as in Matt. vii. 25-27, where a certain degree of good-will toward the truth is assumed in the foolish, from their putting themselves in the relation of hearers, and even attempting to build.

3. "Here there is a controversy . . ." ; the same as that concerning the import of the wedding-garment (Notes, Chapter XII.). The Reformers maintained that the lamps of the virgins were the outer deeds of Christianity, and that what the foolish virgins lacked, was the inner spirit of life, the living faith; the Romanist reversed the whole, and

affirmed that what they had was faith, but a faith without works—that they were not careful to nourish the lamp of faith, which they bore in sight of men, with deeds of light done for and in sight of God. It is needless to remark in what different senses the two parties use the word *faith*—the Romanist as the outward profession of the truth; the reformers, as the root and living principle of Christian life. But for these opposite uses of the same term, the two interpretations would not be incapable of a fair reconciliation.

4. The coming of the bridegroom: The love, the earnest longing of the first Christians, made them to assume it to be close at hand; when they died, the kingdom was indeed come unto them. While the matter was left in this uncertainty, it was yet important that after the expectations of the first ages of the Church had proved to be ungrounded, those who examined the Scriptures should find intimations that this might probably be the case; of these there are many, and this passage is one.

5. *The virgins all slumbered,* or nodded; next, they *slept* profoundly.

6. *Trimmed their lamps.* Ward describing the parts of a marriage ceremony in India, of which he was an eye-witness, says: "After waiting two or three hours, at length near midnight it was announced, 'Behold, the bridegroom cometh; go ye out to meet him.' All now lighted their lamps, and ran to take their stations in the procession; *some of them had lost their lights and were unprepared, but it was then too late to seek them,* and the procession moved forward."

7. *Our lamps are going out.* The hand-lamp was small; even the lamps used at a festival, which would be larger, needed to be replenished if kept burning long into the night.

8. *Went in with him to the marriage.* Comp. Milton's "Sonnet to a Virtuous Young Lady," where there is constant allusion to this portion of the parable.

In early times, and in the middle ages, this parable was a very favorite subject of Christian art. It may be added that it was a favorite subject for the *mysteries* in the middle ages.

CHAPTER XIV.

1. *From him that hath not shall be taken* . . . Chrysostom: "As a fountain from which water is continually drawn forth, is thereby rather purified, and bubbles up the more, but being stanched, fails altogether; so [with] the spiritual gift and word of doctrine." Augustine, applying 2 Kings iv.: "So, dearly beloved brethren, love increases as long as it is imparted, and therefore we ought industriously to seek vessels into which we can pour the oil—the vessels of love are human beings."

CHAPTER XV.

1. "It is not of course meant . . ."; as when it is said, *the earth bringeth forth fruit of herself,* this does not exclude the rain, and sun, and all other favorable circumstances.

2. "Our Lord's object . . . to exclude the continuous agency of the sower," *i. e.,* of the same kind as he exercises at the first.

CHAPTER XVI.

1. "To all this . . ." Note, "which *was*"—not, which *had been* "a sinner;" and again, "She *is* a sinner," and also, "Thy sins *are* forgiven."

The belief in the indentity of Mary *Magdalene* and this woman has impressed itself on the very language of Christendom; but without good reason.

2. "That a woman . . ." "At a dinner at the consul's house at Damietta, we were much interested in observing a custom of the country. In the room where we were received, besides the divan on which we sat, there were seats all round the walls. Many came in and took their places on those side-seats, uninvited and yet unchallenged. They spoke to those at the table on business or the news of the day, and our host spoke freely to them. We afterwards saw the same custom at Jerusalem."— Narr. of a Miss. of Inquiry to the Jews from the Ch. of Scotland in 1839.

As a specimen of notions of holiness, like Simon's, current among the Jews, a commentator on Prov. v. 8 puts this very question: "How far must one keep away from a harlot?" Rabbi Chasda answers: "Four cubits." And again, various rabbies are extolled for their precautions in keeping lepers at a distance; for ex., by flinging stones at them if they come too near. Gregory the Great: "True righteousness has compassion; false righteousness, disdain."

3. "There is . . . ; faith, and not love, is the prerequisite for forgiveness;" comp. v. 50, "thy *faith* hath saved thee." In the parable, he who owed the large debt is not forgiven it as freely as the other debtor, because of his greater *previous* love; but, on the contrary, the sense of a larger debt remitted, makes him *afterwards* love his creditor more. The parable, then, is not in favor of the Romish theology.

Let me quote, were it only with the hope of bringing it before one reader hitherto ignorant of it, the following passage on the attempt thus to substitute charity for faith in the justification of man. "Sin is the disease. What is the remedy? Charity? Pshaw! Charity, in the large apostolic sense of the term, is the health, the state to be obtained by the use of the remedy, not the sovereign balm itself—faith of grace—faith in the God-manhood, the cross, the mediation, the perfected righteousness of Jesus, to the utter rejection and abjuration of all righteousness of our own! Faith alone is the restorative. The Romish scheme is preposterous; it puts the rill before the spring. Faith is the source,—charity, that is, the whole Christian life, is the stream from it. It is quite childish to talk of faith being imperfect without charity, as wisely might you say that a fire, however bright and strong, was imperfect without heat; or that the sun, however cloudless, is imperfect without beams. The true answer would be: It is not faith, but utter reprobate faithlessness." —*Coleridge.*

In the *Bustan* of the famous Persian poet Saadi, there is a story which seems an echo of this evangelical history. Jesus, while on earth, was once entertained in the cell of a monk of eminent reputation for sanctity; in the same city dwelt a youth sunk in every sin, "whose heart was so black that Satan himself shrank back from it in horror." This last presently appeared before the cell of the monk, and, as smitten by the very presence of the Divine prophet, began to lament with tears the sins of his past life, and implore pardon and grace. The monk indignantly interrupted him, demanding how he dare to appear in his presence and in that of God's holy prophet; assured him that for him it was in vain to seek forgiveness; and in proof how inexorably he considered his lot was fixed for hell, exclaimed, "My God, grant me but one thing, that I may stand far from this man on the judgment day." On this Jesus spoke. "It shall be even so: the prayer of both is granted. This sinner has sought mercy and grace, and has not sought them in vain —his sins are forgiven—his place shall be in Paradise at the last day. But this monk has prayed that he may never stand near this sinner— this prayer too is granted: hell shall be his place; for there this sinner shall never come."

CHAPTER XVII.

1 "Who is my neighbor?" It is striking to see this question of the narrow-hearted scribe, reappearing in one who would think that they had little in common. *Emerson's Essays:* "Do not tell me, as a good man did to-day, of my obligation to put all poor men in good situations. Are they *my* poor? I tell thee, thou foolish philanthropist, that I grudge the dollar, the dime, the cent, I give *to such men as do not belong to me, and to whom I do not belong.* There is a class of persons to whom by all spiritual affinity I am bought and sold; for them I will go to prison, if need be; but your miscellaneous popular charities . . ."

2. *A Samaritan.* It is very curious how the notion that the Samaritans are a mingled people, of two elements, one heathen, one Israelitish, should have found way of late even into learned books. Christian antiquity saw in them a people of unmingled heathen blood, and the expositors of two hundred years ago are quite clear of the mistake.

3. *I will repay thee.* "I" is emphatic: Trouble not the poor man on that score; or, Fear not to be a loser.

4. Of course, this deeper interpretation was not meant for the lawyer, but for the (then) future Church. It was held by most of the Fathers.

5. "We might say . . . ;" *i. e.,* if absolutely needful to give a precise meaning to the oil and wine.

CHAPTER XVIII.

1. Stella remarks that by God's delay in answering prayer it is seen who will prove but as the leopard, which, if it does not attain its prey at the first spring, turns sullenly back, and cannot be induced to repeat the attempt.

CHAPTER XIX.

1. That love of the world, which, keeping itself within the limits of decency, yet takes all the affections of the heart from God—against that men have need to be continually warned, and such a warning is here; not against unrighteousness, but against covetousness.—He desired Christ to be an umpire—such only the original means. It is decidedly best to take *life,* in v. 15, as man's true life — his blessedness: so ever in Scripture.

2. "Thou hast barns . . ." Augustine: "Suppose a friend should enter thy house, and find that thou hadst lodged thy fruits on a damp floor, and he should advise, 'Brother, thou losest the things which thou hast gathered with great labor; in a few days they will corrupt.' 'And what, brother, shall I do?' 'Raise them to a higher room.' Thou wouldst listen to him, and thou wilt not listen to Christ."

3. *Shall be required of thee.* The Jewish doctors taught that Gabriel drew gently out with a kiss the souls of the righteous from their mouths.

CHAPTER XX.

1. *"Sinners* above all others;" literally, *debtors,* with a reference to Luke xii. 58, 59. (Comp. Matt. v. 25, 26; xviii. 24, etc.)

2. "Doubtless this is true of men's lives as well." There are critical moments to which all the future is linked, times of gracious visitation which it is of the deepest importance to observe and improve.—An Arabian writer gives as a receipt for a barren palm-tree, that its owner, accompanied by a friend, go with a hatchet, and giving the stem three blows with the back of it, declare to his friend his purpose of cutting it down. He intercedes for and saves it, and the tree will be certainly fruitful that year.

CHAPTER XXI.

"Perhaps . . ." Comp. Note 3, Chapter XII. Comp. this parable and that in Matt. xxii., and observe in what consistent keeping all the minor circumstances are arranged in each. There, a *king* has armies, and also whole bands of servants, and not merely a single one; the refusal to accept *his* invitation was rebellion, etc.

CHAPTER XXII.

1. "When St. Luke . . ." : so the original indicates.

There is no image upon which the early Church seems to have dwelt with greater delight than this of Christ as the good Shepherd bringing home His lost sheep. Very many gems, seals, etc., represent Him as bringing back a lost sheep on His shoulders. In Tertullian's time, it was painted on the communion chalice; so in bas-reliefs on sarcophagi, and paintings in the catacombs. Sometimes He is sitting as if weary; and this representation always occupies the place of honor, the centre of the vault or tomb.

CHAPTER XXIV.

1. "Publicans," Jews; if not all, yet far the greater number, in Judea. Comp. Luke xix. 9.

2. *He began* . . ., literally, "He began *himself* to be in want;" the famine reached even to him.

3. "We may suppose he *did* eat them . . ." So Calvin.

Bernard: "Foolish sons of Adam, by devouring the husks of swine, ye feed not your hungering souls, but the hunger itself of your souls."

4. *When he was yet a great way off* . . . Eastern proverb: "If a man draws near to God an inch, God will draw near to him an ell;" or as Von Hammer gives it: "Who approaches me a span, to him do I make haste an ell; and who comes to meet me, to him do I make haste in leaps."

5. The ring, too, may be the pledge of betrothal. Comp. Hos. ii. 19, 20, and indeed the whole chapter.

6. *Safe and sound;* the *servant's* words: the *father* has a deeper joy —his son has come back a different man (v. 32).

7. We must place the emphasis on *with me,* else we shall entirely miss the meaning.

CHAPTER XXV.

1. "He feels . . ." They see, then, in the lowering of the bills the first act of his righteousness, getting over its dishonesty by giving it altogether a mystical meaning, and so refusing to contemplate it in the letter at all, or in a way which we shall soon notice.—"Rahab the *harlot;*" Comp. Matt. x. 3; xxvi. 6; Tit. iii. 13.—The two debtors are plainly representatives here of many more; just as but *three* servants are named out of the ten, Luke xix. 13.—To one he remits half, to the other the fifth of his **debt; by** these different proportions teaching us, say many, that charity is not to be a blind profuseness.

The transaction was plainly not with the debtors apart from each other, as is indicated by "And—*thou?*" v. 7.

2. "There are martyrs of the devil . . ." There is a story of an Egyptian eremite, which illustrates this—chancing to see a dancing girl, he was moved to tears. Being asked the reason, he replied, That she should be at such pains to please men in her sinful vocation; and we in our holy calling use so little diligence to please God.

3. "This is the meaning given, though *too vaquely,"*—as by Calvin, who says: The sum of this parable is that we are to deal kindly and generously with our neighbors, so that when we come to the judgment the fruit of our liberality may return to us. If this be all, why an *unjust* steward? Yet this was the point mainly, often exclusively, made by the early Church writers—liberal almsgiving. So Irenæus, Augustine, Athanasius. And so also Erasmus, Luther, and many more.

4. "Mammon" would, I believe, be more correctly spelled with a single *m.*

5. "Others say . . ." Sirac. xxvii. 2: "As a nail sticketh fast between the joinings of the stones, so doth sin stick close between buying and selling." Cajetan: "Mammon *of unrighteousness,* because rarely or never is there wealth in whose accumulation or management there has not occurred sin, either on the part of its possessors, or their agents, or their ancestors."

6. The use of *adikos* ("unrighteous") for "false" runs through the whole Septuagint. Thus Deut. xix. 16.—"In the moment . . ." The existence of property has ever been strongly felt as a witness for the selfishness of man. But with all this, we must not forget that the attempt prematurely to realize this or any other little fragment or corner of the kingdom of God apart from the rest—the corruption of man's heart remaining unremoved and being either overlooked or denied—has ever been one of the most fruitful sources of the worst mischiefs,

7. *That when ye fail.* It may perhaps be a question whether this should not be "that when *it* fails," *i. e.,* the mammon. In the case Seneca has a striking parallel: "Marc Antony, when he saw his fortune passing over to another and nothing left for himself, exclaimed, finely: *Whatso-*

ever I have given away, this I have. These are sure riches that will abide in one spot, in whatsoever fickleness of fortune."

8. *Everlasting habitations,* thus tacitly contrasted with the temporary shelter which was all that the steward could secure; also perhaps, with the temporary stewardship of every man here. An ancient writer supposes the unjust steward to have been the Apostle Paul thrust out by God of his Judaism, then making himself a reception in many hearts by preaching the Gospel; and a modern author affirms the Lord Himself to have been meant!

CHAPTER XXVI.

1. "It is most important . . ."; if we conceive of its primary purpose as to warn against the abuse of riches, it will neither satisfactorily cohere with the remaining discourse, nor will the parable itself possess that unity of purpose so characteristic of our Lord's parables—it will seem to have a double point.

2. "The extreme costliness of the purple dye," *i. e.,* the true sea-purple, but a few drops of dyeing liquid being found in each fish; what fish exactly is not now known.

"Byssus." Pliny tells of a kind exchanged for its weight in gold.

3. "His name . . ." Augustine: "Seems he not to you to have been reading from that book where he found the name of the poor man written, but found not the name of the rich; for that book is the book of life?"

4. "Lazarus" It is a striking witness of the impression this parable has made, that *lazar* should have passed into so many languages, losing altogether its signification as a proper name.

5. Luther: "Behold, he, who while living had not even one man for a friend, is suddenly honored with the ministry not of one angel but of many."

6. Chrysostom: "For as on the stage some enter, assuming the masks of kings and captains, physicians and orators, philosophers and soldiers, being in truth nothing of the kind; so also in the present life, wealth and proverty are only masks. As then, when thou sittiest in the theatre, and beholdest one playing below who sustains the part of a king, thou dost not count him happy, nor esteemest him a king, nor desirest to be such as he; but knowing him to be one of the common people, a ropemaker or a blacksmith, or some such a one as this, thou dost not esteem him happy for his mask, and his robe's sake, nor judgest of his condition from these, but holdest him cheap for the meanness of his true condition: so also, here sitting in the world as in a theatre, and beholding men playing as on a stage, when thou seest many rich, count them not to be truly rich, but to be wearing the masks of rich. For as he, who in the stage plays the king or captain, is often a slave, or one who sells figs or grapes in the market, so also this rich man is often in reality poorest of all. For if thou strip him of his mask, and unfold his conscience, and scrutinize his inward parts, thou wilt there find a great penury of virtue; thou wilt find him to be indeed the most abject of men. And as in the theatre, when evening is come and the spectators are departed, and the players are gone forth thence, having laid aside their

masks and their dresses, then they who before showed as kings and captains to all, appear now as they truly are; so now, when death approaches and the audience is dismissed, all, laying aside the masks of wealth and poverty, depart from hence, and, being judged only by their works, appear some indeed truly rich, but some poor; and some glorious, but others without honor." Arndt compares such as the rich man in the parable to camels and mules, who carry all day silken vestments, gems, perfumes, and generous wines, but as soon as they reach the stall at night, are unladen, and show nothing but the marks of blows.

7. "Such was . . ." Thus in the Jewish books the scholar of an eminent rabbi found his master one day in extreme affliction, and began to laugh, while all the other scholars were weeping around him. Being upbraided, he answered that he had often feared lest his master was receiving his portion in this world, but now seeing him afflicted, he took courage again.

8. *A great gulf* there, not merely, *fixed* there.

9. *If they hear not* . . . In effect saying: A far greater act than you desire would fail to produce a far less effect: you suppose that wicked men would repent on the return of a spirit; I tell you they would not even be persuaded by the rising of one from the dead. It is a pity that we have not "*if* one" in v. 31 as in v. 30.

10. "When the Gentile Church . . ." Nor are we to expect, before its judgment, any startling summons to rouse it—any novel sign.

CHAPTER XXVII.

1. *Say, we are unprofitable servants.* Bengel: "Wretched is he whom the Lord calls an unprofitable servant (Matt. xxv. 30)—blessed, he who calls himself so."

CHAPTER XXVIII.

1. This parable is addressed to the disciples, and stands in closest relation with what has gone immediately before, with the description of the sufferings of the last times, when even the disciples "shall desire to see one of the days of the Son of man, and shall not see it" (Luke xvii. 22).

2. "In this precept . . ." Origen; "The whole life of the faithful should be one connected prayer." St. Basil: "Prayer should be the salt which is to salt everything besides." Augustine: "There is another interior prayer without intermission, and that is the longing of thy heart.—Thy continual desire is thy continual voice. Thou wilt be silent, if thou leave off to love. The coldness of love is the silence of the heart —the fervency of love is the cry of the heart!"

3. "This judge . . ."; and he dared to avow this contempt to himself.

4. "How fitly, then . . ." It would be a very imperfect view of those cries for deliverance, occurring so often in the Psalms and Prophets, to refer them to any particular and transient outward persecutions. The world is always, consciously or unconsciously, by flattery or by hostile violence, oppressing God's people; and Satan evermore seeking to hinder the manifestation of the life of God in them.

5. "From the Evil One"—the source and centre of all evil. The analogy of other passages, Matt. xiii. 19, 38, 39; Eph. vi. 16; 2 Thess. iii. 3, would lead us so to translate; and so was it interpreted in the Greek Church.

6. *He said* . . . The endeavor to obtain help or redress by long-continued crying and mere importunity—to extort thus a boon or a right —is quite in the spirit of the East.

7. "The certainty . . . on their election;" Comp. Daniel xii. 1.

8. *Shall he find faith?* or rather *that* faith, the faith which does not faint in prayer, with allusion to v. 1.

9. "All help . . ." The lateness of the help Zechariah (xiv. 1-5) describes, under the images of the old theocracy—Jerusalem shall be already taken, the enemy within its walls and spoiling, when the Lord shall come forth.

CHAPTER XXIX.

1. "The last . . ." Augustine finds a yet closer connection: "Because faith belongs not to the proud but to the humble, He added a parable about humility in contrast with pride." He had seen in some of His followers spiritual pride and contempt for others.—This Pharisee, with all who pride themselves because of their victory over certain temptation, is wittily likened by Gregory the Great to Eleazar, who killed the elephant, but was himself crushed by its falling body (1 Macc. vi. 46).

2. "Acknowledgment . . ." Augustine: "Had he then no sins to confess? Yes, but—he was like a patient on the table of a surgeon, who should show his sound limbs, and cover his hurts. But let God cover thy hurts, and not thou. Let Him cover and cure them; for under the covering of the physician the wound is healed, under the covering of the sufferer, it is only concealed; and concealed from whom? From Him to Whom all things are known!"

3. *Not so much as his eyes:* far less, then, his hands and his countenance, which yet would be usually lifted up in prayer (1 Tim. ii. 8; 1 Kings viii. 54; Heb. xii. 12; Ps. xxviii. 2), which no doubt the Pharisee had lifted up in his.

4. "Christ does not mean . . ." It is characteristic that this should be denied by nearly all the chief Romanist commentators, though in fact this is the very truth which the parable is to teach.

CHAPTER XXX.

1. "In the great Roman Empire . . ." Thus Herod the Great was at first no more than a subordinate officer in Judea, and flying to Rome before Antigonus, was there declared by the Senate, through Antony's influence, King of the Jews. Archelaus, his son, too, had personally to wait on Augustus in Rome before inheriting his father's dominions.

2. "This nobleman . . ." Either supposition, it is true, would suit *Christ's* case.

3. *We will not* . . .Exactly thus, a faction of the Jews, in the case of Archelaus, sent ambassadors to the court of Augustus to accuse him there, and if possible prevent his elevation.

4. *Occupy, i. e.,* employ in trading.

5. "If we find . . ." The parable is equally capable of the narrower and the wider interpretation.—"A speaking of great things against Him;" not merely disobedience but defiance.

6. "The rewards . . ." Contrast Matt. xxv. 14-30, where the master is but a private man, and gives therefore humbler rewards.

7. "Those who stand by . . ." The servant not needing his napkin for its proper use (in the *sweat* . . . Gen. iii. 19), naturally uses it to wrap up his pound.

8. "The words . . ." As there is love in the Old Testament, so fear and that which should awaken it in the New.